Jackson Luis Schirigatti

Designing and Managing Software Projects with Quality

Jackson Luis Schirigatti

Designing and Managing Software Projects with Quality

A Methodological, Metrological and People approach: PMI, PM Mind Map, Scrum, Lean, XP, Kanban and Hybrids

ScienciaScripts

Imprint
Any brand names and product names mentioned in this book are subject to trademark, brand or patent protection and are trademarks or registered trademarks of their respective holders. The use of brand names, product names, common names, trade names, product descriptions etc. even without a particular marking in this work is in no way to be construed to mean that such names may be regarded as unrestricted in respect of trademark and brand protection legislation and could thus be used by anyone.

Cover image: www.ingimage.com

This book is a translation from the original published under ISBN 978-620-2-80430-1.

Publisher:
Sciencia Scripts
is a trademark of
International Book Market Service Ltd., member of OmniScriptum Publishing Group
17 Meldrum Street, Beau Bassin 71504, Mauritius
Printed at: see last page
ISBN: 978-620-2-84115-3

Summary

1. Evolution of Quality 2

2. Software development methodologies...12

  2.1 Traditional software processes..19

    2.1.1 Software specification stage 20

    2.1.2 Software Development Project Stage 23

    2.1.3 Software implementation step 37

    2.1.4 Software validation (testing) stage 40

    2.1.5 Software evolution stage...41

  2.2 Traditional software development models...41

    2.2.1 Cascade Model...41

    2.2.2 Incremental Model 43

    2.2.3 Prototyping Model 46

    2.2.4 Boehm Spiral Model..49

    2.2.5 RUP Model - Rational Unified Process...51

  2.3 Agile software development methodologies.......................................57

    2.3.1 Extreme Programming 58

    2.3.2 *Scrum* - fast software management..61

    2.2.3 Proper selection of agile software development methodologies 66

    2.3.4 Agile methodologies based on industrial production 69

    2.3.5 *Lean* Software Method...74

    2.3.6 *Kanban* method...77

    2.3.7 *Scrumban* method 79

    2.3.8 *Scrumban* + XP Method...81

  2.4 Software Development Project Management 83

    2.4.1 Relevance of projects 91

    2.4.2 Areas of Knowledge 92

    2.4.3 Reasons and benefits of project management.................................96

2.4.4 Managing the scope of a project 113

2.4.5 Time management of a project 131

2.4.6 Managing the cost of a project 140

2.5 Software Metrics 145

2.5.1 Software measurement process 148

2.6 People and communication management 158

2.6.1 Agile teams 173

In addition to growing and surviving, organizations need to gain competitive advantage through the development of products and services, especially in a scenario of socio-political-economic change. For this it is necessary to innovate more and more to improve quality, productivity, efficiency and effectiveness in organizational processes, products, services and especially in software development, thus ensuring the achievement of strategic objectives. In this context projects are essential in the planning, control, execution and delivery of tasks, both in production processes and software processes. Combining these processes is not an easy task, being necessary the software manager or engineer to better understand how the software production process can be integrated with a traditional or agile project approach.

1. Quality Evolution

It was from the evolution of quality that the methods and their studies (methodologies) were applied the activities of software development and software projects. Thus, it is necessary initially to understand how the evolution of quality occurred during history and how to seek efficiency in industrial and software production activities.

The concern with the quality already very old, and it has been evolving in steps not so wide nowadays. Oliveira (2012) comments that this concern dates from 2150 BC. Through the code of Hamurabi (set of law, Fig.1), demonstrating concern with the durability and functionality of homes produced at the time. In which if the constructions were not solid enough, the builder was sacrificed.

Fig. 1 - Hamurabi Code - set of laws written on a monument
Source: commons.wikimedia.org (2020)

The history of quality is divided into four eras by David Garvin (1952-2017): The first era, called the era of inspection. It happened in the middle ages by artisans, producers and inspectors. For Oliveira (2012) it happened a little before the Industrial Revolution, a period that reached its peak. In this era the product was inspected by the producer and the customer and searched for eventual manufacturing defects, without the existence of a pre-established metrology. In the following era, the inspection control was improved through statistical techniques (statistical quality control) through sampling (randomly selected products) and no longer by product to product. This was due to a large production scale and high worldwide demand, making individualized inspection inconvenient and costly. Some authors make a different division, where the next era, the third era of quality, is the one we are living in. As Oliveira (2012) calls it, the era of total quality, where the production process is controlled and the whole company is responsible for quality assurance. The table below illustrates a division into four historical eras.

Table 1 - Classification and characteristics of the quality ages

The age of quality	Features
First Age **(formalisation in the 1920s)**	<ul><li>Manual production.</li><li>Limited quantity.</li><li>With industrialization in the 1920s there was a formalization of inspection in production.</li><li>Emergence of templates, matrices, detection of "non-conformity" and verification of the attempt to fit non-compatible parts.</li></ul>
Second Age (30s and 40s)	<ul><li>Decade 30 and 40, a greater quality control due to industrialization intensified by World War II.</li><li>Quality control carried out by the Statistical Quality Control - CEP (reports and mention in 1922).</li><li>First scientific works Shewhart (1931 - principles of quality, Dodge, Roming and Deming).</li><li>Process control charts, sampling plans.</li></ul>
Third Age (1960s)	<ul><li>It occurs from the 1960s onwards.</li><li>The quality was not only of the technicians (quality department), but a work of all sectors.</li><li>The era of quality assurance (Deming - 1950 - quality foundations).</li><li>It considers the quantification of quality costs.</li></ul>

	• It includes the study of reliability. • It considers a zero defects programme. • Expansion of the managerial aspect of quality, but still with an aspect in the prevention of defects.
Fourth Era (to the present day)	• Called "the new era" today. • It considers a strong link between quality and profitability. • It establishes quality from the consumer's point of view. • It has a commitment from top management to quality. • Establishes a total quality control (TQC), that is, all areas with results in quality, aiming at cost reduction and customer satisfaction. • In 1980 the consolidation of the increase of three decades prior to the quality logic is carried out: TQM - total quality management. • Quality must be translated for competitors rather than internal standards. • Understanding what quality means to the customer and producing according to this orientation. • The above concepts are contemplated (interdepartmental coordination, zero defects program, concern with quality costs and statistical control tools) = uniform product. • The focus is not on defect detection and "non-conformities" (contemplates but does not focus on) but on strategic management.

The third era is related to quality management in a systemic way and its security. The fourth historical era, called the "new era" by the classification presented in the table, is related to total quality control (TQC) and has a strategic rather than operational vision.

We can also summarize each quality era in six main characteristics such as vision, emphasis, methods, the role of the professional, approach/orientation and the quality officer, as shown in table 2 below:

Table 2 - Classification and characteristics of the quality ages

The age of quality/	First Age	Second Age	Third Age	Fourth Era
Vision	A problem to be solved	A problem to be solved	A problem can be solved proactively	Strategic impact; A competitive opportunity;
Emphasis	Product uniformity	Uniformity of products with reduced inspection	The whole production chain, from project to market, contribution of the functional groups.	The market and consumer needs;
Method	Calibration and measurement	Technical statistical tools	Quality programmes	Strategic Planning; Setting Goals by mobilizing the organization.
Role of the Professional	Inspection, classification and counting.	Problem solving and application of statistical methods.	Quality measurement and planning	Everyone in the organisation with top management exercising strong leadership.
Guidance /approach	Inspection Quality	Engineering & Manufacturing Department	Quality is built	Quality is built
Responsible for quality	Inspection Department	Quality is controlled	All departments; Senior management involved only in the design, planning and execution of quality policies.	Everyone in the organisation with top management exercising strong leadership.

Total quality management is based on principles such as cost of quality, reliability engineering, zero defect, participation of all its members and long-term success for customer satisfaction and benefits for all in the organisation. But what would quality really be and would it apply to software processes? Let's look at a detail about the concept of quality and its application to the software process.

Nowadays there is an intense and constant movement in the search for quality in all areas of knowledge. Everything demands quality, in production or service, in the maintenance of a machine or software, in the preparation of a food, in the phases of a project, in the development of a software, in the construction of a building, etc. For Oliveira (2012, p.3) "organizations have to produce quality products, no longer as a differentiation strategy in the market, but as a condition of pre-existence". The concept of quality is linked to fair price, correct functioning, overcoming expectations, it is also here that it does well and pleases or satisfies us. Quality is a set of characteristics of a product or service which gives it satisfaction requirements for the needs of the customer. As for the quality of information technology, it is expressly necessary like any other area or product or service, whereas information technology deals with the technological component hardware and software for the input, storage, processing and output of information.

The importance of quality for software is paramount in its organisation and coding (compilation, documentation, establishment of standards and quality processes). The quality of a software is directly related to the quality levels of the processes involved in development and implementation. Software engineering is an area of information technology responsible for these software construction processes. These processes include techniques used in specification, design, development and testing, aiming at a quality product, that is, one that meets the expectations for which it is being developed in an organized, productive and most economical way. In the agile methodologies of software production, (specifically in the fast teams of *Scrum* and *XP*) part of the success is due to the fact that the teams are consistently producing work of higher quality. Without errors, or zero defects, any team can move forward quickly and consistently. The quality is higher because it works at a constant pace avoiding sloppiness. Quality is also increased through various development practices with pair programming, refactoring and a strong emphasis on early and automated testing. Quality is important, but it costs us time and money - too much time to get the level of software quality we really want. There is no doubt that quality has a price, not only for users, but for the entire organization that created it.

Software standards play a very important role in software quality management, as standards have been selected for use, project specific processes and must be defined to monitor the use of these standards and verify that they have been followed up. In Fig. 2, below, we illustrate process-based quality through continuous improvement. Where the quality process is defined, the product developed and the product quality evaluated according to the defined standards. If it is not in compliance the process should be improved, if it is in compliance the process should be standardised. This would be a cycle of continuous quality improvement, called PDCA or Deming (Plan - Do - Check - Act) wheel, i.e. plan, execute, evaluate and adjust. Realize that every time the quality indicator is in non-compliance (below the quality target), the process needs to be improved, however the process standardization is not watertight. Any change in the product the process must be redefined at the beginning of the process.

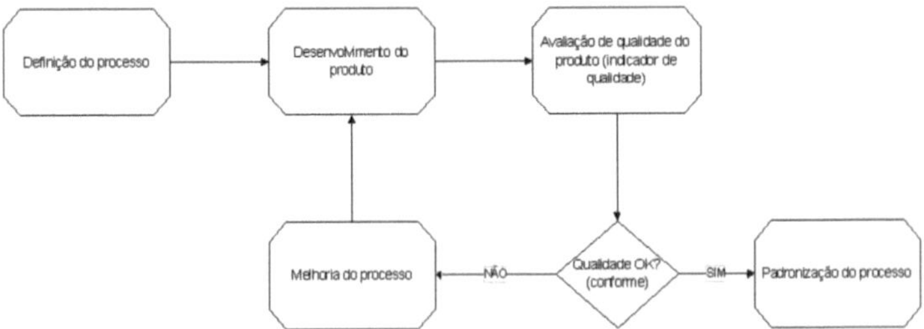

Fig. 2 - Process standardization process using an improvement approach

The famous process of continuous improvement, the PDCA is used in industry operations, administration, project management and other areas. The continuous improvement cycle (plan, execute, check and act) was developed by Shewhart and popularized by Deming, becoming one of the most powerful jargons of business management and total quality. In project and process management of any kind, Fig. 3 below illustrates the PDCA in the project or process management process. The planning phase (Plan) in the case of activities or processes must be planned (which should be ideal), or a process must be studied and planned for improvement. The execution phase (Do) concerns the realisation of process activities as defined in the planning phase. Implementation is the change. In the Check or Audit phase, the metrics and quality indicators planned to measure the process activities are verified. This phase is the observation of defects. In the action phase the causes that are causing the deviations (non-conformities) are identified. After this identification, the planning phase is returned to plan new processes, correcting the deviations. This phase is of studies of the results to start the new planning cycle.

9

Figure 3 - PDCA or Deming cycle

Source: commons.wikimedia.org / Tagimaguitar - CC BY-SA 3.0 (2012)

With each Plan, Do, Check and Act cycle executed, new improvements are made to the processes, achieving greater efficiency. Each time the PDCA cycle "rotates" a stage, called "maturity of processes", is raised.

1.1 Quality in software development: prescriptive and adaptive methods:

With regard to quality in software development, methods can be either prescriptive or adaptive, depending on the software design or the need for the prescription dosage of the documentation required to obtain quality in development, maintenance and use. It is important to check whether the methods are more prescriptive or adaptive for adaptations to the context of the projects and for the necessary combinations to other approaches. Prescriptive methods (traditional methods) are the most explicit in terms of roles, activities and artefacts. Adaptive methods (agile methods) establish constant states of change, transformation and aiming at a state of continuous improvement. When the method is more adaptive, more flexible and adherent it will be for different contexts. When the methods are more prescriptive, they are more context specific.

The prescriptive methods, have too much documentation, however sometimes software engineers consider the standards too prescriptive and not really relevant to the technical activity of software development. You should keep in mind that this relationship depends on the type of software design or process that occurs. Critical projects of complex systems should have a more prescriptive than adaptive focus.

Fig. 4 below illustrates the prescriptive and adaptive methods. You can see that the RUP and XP have a larger volume of prescriptions (circle diameter), than Scrum and Kanban. For complex projects with large teams, prescriptions are necessary for the predictability of the risk factor. Ideally, you should first understand the context before choosing and combining software development and project management methodologies.

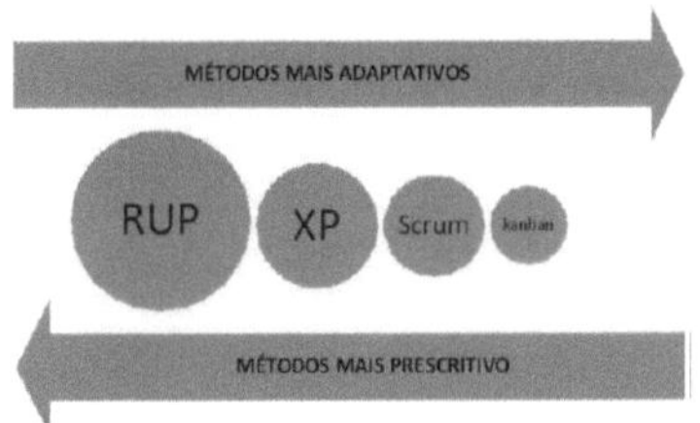

Figure 4 - Software development methods - more and less prescriptive and adaptive

Within the context of prescriptive to adaptive methodologies, traditional and agile software development methodologies are related respectively. Let's look at the concepts of these methodologies in the software development process.

2. Software development methodologies

Figure 5 - methodology - sequence of activities
Source: freepik / vectorpouch (2020)

For Koscianski and Soares (2007, p.190), "a software development methodology is a set of activities that assist in software production. The result of these activities is a product that reflects the way the process was conducted". However, a set of activities is called a process, in this case a software development methodology uses software production processes. Engholm Jr. (2010, p.42) comments that process is a sequential and peculiar set of actions aimed at achieving a goal. It is used to create, invent, design, transform, produce, control, maintain and use products or systems.

The processes are linked to the activities and procedures of a company's employees or collaborators. These processes are composed of work routines, called work instructions. A payroll system, production and control planning, storage, ordering and other functions are linked to organisational processes. Processes are composed of 'input' information or raw materials; 'processing' calculations or transformation of information or raw materials; 'output' information, results or finished products; 'resources' personnel or finance; and 'rules and standards' such as policies, work instructions, norms, regulations, etc., as shown in Fig. 6.

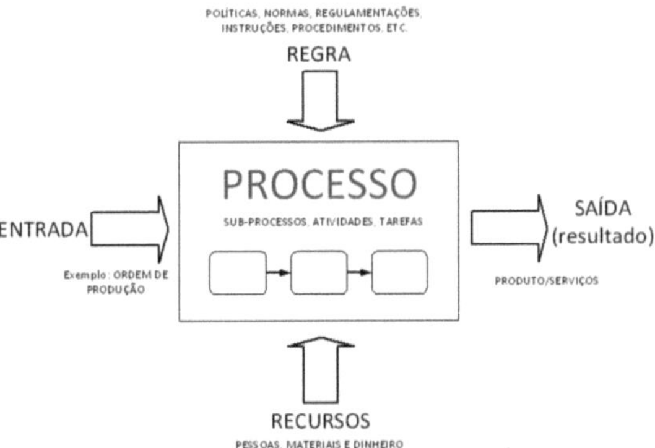

Fig. 6 - Representation of a process

We can cite some characteristics about the case, listed by Engholm Jr. (2010, p.43): "is triggered/initiated by an external event; encompasses all activities necessary to provide the appropriate results in response to the event that initiated it; has performance indicators for which measurable objectives can be set, and performance, evaluated, [...] etc.", composed of activities and these broken down by functional routines or procedures, reaching as much detail as possible of the activity, i.e., "how to do the procedure", governed by determined norms, specifications or standards and executed by technological or human resources.

The activity is a set of tasks that occur within a process or sub-process. A task is defined as any activity performed by a person in his or her work within the organisation. It is the smallest possible unit within the division of labour in an organisation, it represents the smallest division of the organisation's process. But the task can reach an even smaller division, such as routines, procedures or work instructions representing times and movements. These movements are called elementary movements or *therbligs* (table 3):

Table 3 - elementary movements.

13

| 1. Plan |
| 2. Choose |
| 3. Pick up |
| 4. Transport |
| 5. Position |
| 6. Separate |
| 7. Use |
| 8. Inspecional |

The analysis and study of these procedures, in relation to time and their movements can increase the efficiency of the worker (correct use of available resources).

A process has an organisational structure through a hierarchy, where the level of detail with which the work is being addressed is represented. The macroprocess figure showed the various levels of detail and the possible nomenclatures. The macro process level is defined in the methodology as the lowest level of detail and includes macro areas of the organisation, such as manufacturing, commercial, engineering, information technology, etc. But they can be defined with as little detail as possible, such as industrial/production, administrative, logistics, customers and suppliers. The macro process is subdivided into sub-processes and these into activities and tasks, according to the need for detailing necessary for the mapping of processes. The division of processes is a question of the need for detailing the process mapping, and only during the application of the methodology it is possible to question this structure.

a) Macro process: it is a process that usually involves more than one function in the organizational structure and has significant impact on the organization as a whole. Example Macro Production Process,

Commercial, Financial, Controlling etc. The level of detail are the processes.

b) Process: is a set of (connected), related and logical activities that take a business event as input, add value (transformation) and produce an output for a client from another internal or external process. The level of detail can be the subprocesses or directly the activities. Example of processes: Managerial, Tributary, Tax, Activities inherent to Legislation, State, ICMS.

c) Sub-process: it is the same as a process, its level of detail being greater than that of the process. It achieves a specific objective in support of the macro-process and contributes to its mission. Example of sub-processes of the ICMS process: Factories and Suppliers, receive NF, Generate Report, Issue Online Guide, Record folder and financial advice.

d) Activity: is a set of tasks that occur within a process or subprocess. They are usually performed by a unit (person or department) to produce a specific result. They constitute the major part by flowcharts. Examples can be the same as for a sub-process.

e) Task: it is the least effort of the process and can be a single element of an activity. They are work instructions of an activity or routines of an activity. Example: work instructions of the activity "Issue Online Guide" (1. receive information from the guide, 2. check information, 3. fill in electronic form, etc.).

Business rules are part of a process, where they guide the processes and subprocesses. They are established by policies, procedures, regulations, laws, standards, etc. A process has business rules, procedures and technical specifications that guide the processes. The needs for business rules exist due to several factors, such as external factors: competitive pressure, complexity of compliance with external regulations, changes in regulations and laws; internal factors: inconsistent or conflicting business rules, difficulty in understanding current rules, difficulty in identifying new business opportunities, etc. A Business Rule is a statement that restricts some aspect of business and represents knowledge of the business. A business rule is a phrase composed of terms, facts, restrictions and derivation. Example:

Term + suit = Customer can place an order.

Restriction = the order may only have one delivery address.

Derivation = when one rule uses the knowledge of another rule.

Example: initial calculation rules of one rule have already been defined in another rule.

Regarding software processes, Sommerville (2011, p.18-19) comments that software production processes can be in different ways, whether for new software developed from scratch or for implementations, but should include four activities, steps or phases fundamental to software engineering: (1) software specification (definitions of functionalities and operation); (2) software design and implementation (production, coding); (3) software validation (validation to ensure customer demands) and (4) software evolution.

The software production processes, also called traditional software development phases, can be defined as (Fig. 7):

a)   Analysis and requirements (software specification);

b)   Project;

(c)   Implementation; (software design and implementation); and

d)   Testing (software validation and evolution).

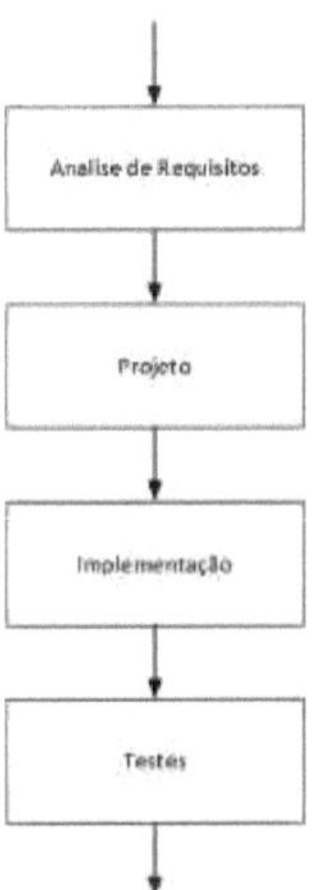

Fig. 7 - Traditional phases of software life cycle development.

According to Royce (1970) apud Koscianski and Soares (2007, p.190), traditional methodologies are also called heavy or document-oriented or strongly prescriptive. These methodologies emerged in a context of software development very different from today's, based only on mainframes and dumb terminals. Still according to Koscianski and Soares (2007, p.190), the first published software development methodology is the so-called cascade methodology or classic model, where it establishes a sequence of steps, we will see more on this study of the principles of software development methodologies.

Today there are many methodologies for software development and management, both traditional and agile, which can be combined for better production efficiency, risk reduction, higher quality and lower cost. An agile methodology has a focus more related to people and the traditional one more related to processes. Not that traditional methodologies are not concerned with people, but are more related to processes and tools. For example, some traditional approaches to project management, such as PMI, focused on processes, currently from its 5th edition, are concerned with the "people" emphasis, inserting in their management processes a new process called "*stakeholders*". Traditional methodologies have a predictive rather than an adaptive approach, the latter characteristic of agile models. The idea of predictive is to predict through plans, the possible risks, course changes in scope, costs and time of the project. In the agile paradigm, there is already a focus that changes will occur anyway, and development can undergo these changes at any time. Agile methodologies bet that it is better to do something simple and unforeseen today, and pay a little more and make the necessary changes tomorrow, than to carry out a planning that consumes a lot of time to predict what will be done. When it comes to generating artifacts in projects that use the classic paradigm, it is possible to generate a large amount of documentation needed to forecast and direct the project, but not that it is mandatory, because everything depends on the security of the project leader and the knowledge regarding similar projects. In the agile paradigm, deliveries are incremental with little or no documentation. In the agile methodology, we rely on versioned deliveries of functionalities prioritized and approved by the client. Another question to be raised is the impersonality of agile paradigm projects, which has been much questioned by several authors. In the agile methodology, the collaboration of the client is essential, not that in the classic methodology it is not, but it requires maturity in the relationship between the organization and the client without signed contracts. For the lack of legal documents can cause some headaches regarding the scope, time and cost and the deliverables of the project. Let's see below more details about traditional software development processes.

2.1 Traditional software processes

The traditional stages of software life cycle development (Fig. 8) is composed of four phases (1) analysis and definition of software requirements or specifications, step for understanding the services required from the system; (2) design and implementation, where the conversion of the specification into an executable system is performed, from modeling (design) to software coding (implementation); (3) validation of the software through tests, with the intention of presenting a functional software that fits the client's specifications; and we can add the phase of (4) evolution of the software that refers to maintenance for the survival of the software.

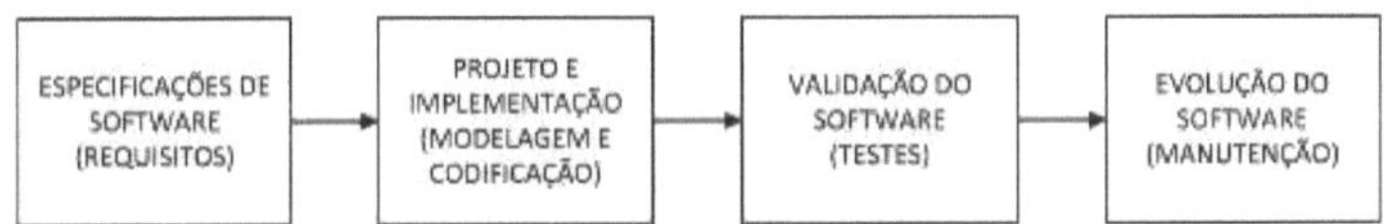

Fig. 8 - Traditional phases of software development.

The software specification phase, this is the moment of understanding the services or product requested by the client, in this case the result generated is a consulting or product (software or systems). Here we must ask the following questions: "is such a service or product feasible for the business?", "is there a budget available to develop the product or service?", "how do you want such a service?", "what are the requirements of the service or product?", "are the desired requirements really defined? Some authors present this phase, also as a feasibility and systems analysis stage. In the feasibility study it is necessary to identify the current deficiencies, set objectives in the new system; generate acceptable scenarios; prepare project charges. In the system analysis activities], develop the environmental model, develop the behavioural model; establish the human-machine limits, perform the cost-benefit analysis (REZENDE, 2005, p.42).

2.1.1 Software specification stage

The software lifecycle begins with the analysis of requirements - the aim of which is to specify which services the proposed system will provide, identify any conditions (time constraints, security and so on) of these services and define how the outside world will interact with the system (BROOKSHEAR, 2013, p.267). For Sommerville (2011, p.24), "this phase also called software specification or requirements engineering is the process of understanding and defining the services required from the system and identifying constraints on system operation and development". Fig. 9 shows the activities of the requirements engineering process, resulting in a requirements documentation. The activities are of: (1) feasibility study; (2) elicitation and analysis of requirements; (3) specification of requirements and (4) validation of requirements.

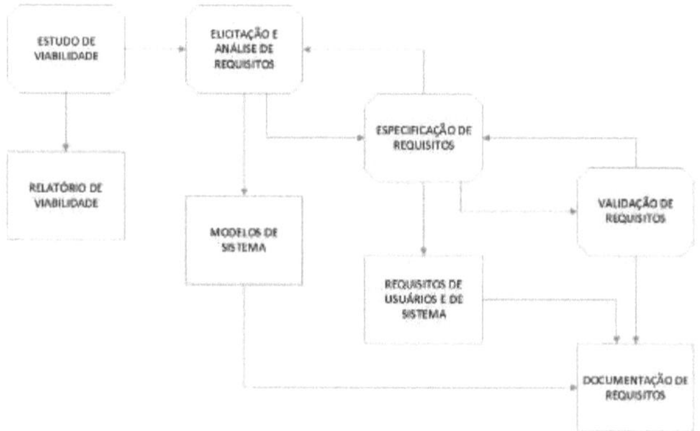

Fig. 9 - process engineering requirements

a) **Feasibility study:** this is the first activity in the requirements engineering process. It is an activity to verify whether the proposed system is feasible from a business and budgetary point of view. If a project management concept is applied, this stage is analysed in the opening and planning phase of the project, where the needs assessment, planning of the scope, time and cost of the project, based on the proposed budget and selected by the project portfolio, is carried out. Some authors also call this stage a needs assessment workflow, where the client's needs, time verification, reliability and cost are identified. For Sommerville (2011, p.25), "a feasibility study should be relatively inexpensive and quick. The result should inform the decision to proceed or not, with a more detailed analysis". The product generated from this activity is a feasibility report.

b) **Elicitation and analysis of requirements:** it is the second activity of the requirements engineering process is elicitation and analysis of requirements. In this activity it is the "discovery of requirements", "survey of requirements", or even as a search or collection of information, through observation, documentation, discussions, etc. The elicitation of requirements is a unique task of business analysis. It is essential that the desired requirements are complete, objective, correct and consistent, because they serve as the basis for the solution to business needs. The requirements elicitation activity is not an isolated activity, requirements are defined during the analysis, specification and validation of requirements. Some techniques for requirements elicitation can be used as brainstorming, interviewing, observation, interface analysis, prototyping, requirements workshop, research and questionnaire. Software requirements are conditions that must be met by a system, product or component of this system, a standard, a specification, or formal documentation. The "requirements of a project" include the needs, wishes and expectations of the sponsor, customer and other parties. Requirements are the wishes of customers with regard to the project that will generate a product or service. The product or service requirements generated by the project are the business rules (standards, conditions), are functionalities of a system or processes (functional and non-functional requirements) desirable.

c) **Specification of requirements:** Requirements specification is the activity of translating the information collected during the analysis activity into a document that defines a set of requirements. These are two types of requirements:

1. user requirements: these are the desired functionalities, what the customer wants in the solution to solve his problem.
2. system requirements: these are the functionalities met according to the customer/user requirements.

"The user requirements for a system, describe the functional and non-functional requirements, so that they are understandable to the users of the system who have no detailed technical knowledge. (SOMMERVILLE, 2011, p. 65).

The functional requirements are those that define the system behaviour, through the Use Case (UML diagram to model systems) that document the inputs, processes and outputs generated. Example: a registration of customers whose access is performed by the customer's CPF, the description of the product must contain the technical specifications governed by a certain technical standard. Non-functional requirements, on the other hand, are composed of characteristics that are not necessarily behavioral, such as usability, reliability, performance and support.

d) **Validation of requirements:** The requirements validation activity is a quality assurance work in the requirements engineering stage that ensures that all specified requirements are aligned with the business requirements. In other words, ensuring that all business needs of stakeholders in the scope of the project are met. For Sommerville (2011, p.25), this activity checks for realism, consistency and completeness. During this process, errors in the requirements document are inevitably discovered, then the document must be modified to correct these problems.

2.1.2 Software Development Project Stage

After the elicitation and requirements analysis step, for example through a use case diagram (UML - Unified Modeling Language) and validations, the software development project phase is the link between the coding and its requirements, aiming to establish a software architecture.

Unified Modeling Language (UML) has a wide use aspect, its main function is the modelling of business rules and system specifications, understanding both the structural aspects of the software and the dynamics. To provide this wide range of application, the language has been defined so that it can be extended and is generic (standardized) enough to deal with different types of systems, avoiding specializations and excessive complexity.

In this sense the need for project standardization is an efficiency factor in the software process. The standardization of projects involves, within a software process, the standardization of modeling, coding and testing for better productivity, efficiency and quality of the software in these steps. Gamma et al. (2000, p. 19) comment that software design standards are those that describe a problem in our environment and the core of the solution, whereas it is possible to use this solution several times. This design pattern is expressed in objects and user-friendly interfaces - in this case, the designs are object-oriented.

A design pattern consists of four elements: (1) the name of the pattern, (2) the problem, (3) the solution, and (4) the consequences, and the name of the pattern corresponds to a reference that we can use to describe a design problem. The element of the problem describes in which situation the pattern will be applied. The solution describes the elements that make up the project standard and their relationships, their responsibilities and collaborations. The consequences are the results and analysis of the advantages and disadvantages of applying the standard (GAMMA et al., 2000, p.19). Kerievsky (2008, p. 54) comments that the use of vision refactoring for standardization helps us to focus cautiously on removing duplication and simplifying the code, making the code communicate its intent. When patterns evolve in a system through refactoring, there is a lower chance of over-projecting with patterns.

Project standards can be classified according to the structure of objects and classes and how they interact in a software application. They are classified into:

1. creation patterns: they help in the independence of the system and how objects are created, composed and represented;

2. structural patterns: they define a pattern of object and class design (simplification and relationship between objects and classes);

3. behavioral patterns: responsible for standardizing the interaction between objects and their responsibilities.

Project standardization focuses on the execution of a reorganization and refactoring task, tending to a reduction in volume and optimization of modeling and coding, since it is possible to standardize objects from their creation in the model - using a standardization model, for example - to their codification with good programming practices. UML (*Unified Modeling Language*), in addition to expressing an object-oriented design, can support itself in modeling a design pattern.

Pressman and Maxim (2016, p.225-226) say that software design is at the technical core of software engineering and is applied whatever the software process model used. Once the software requirements have been analysed and modeled, the software design is the latest software engineering action in the modelling activity and prepares the scenario for construction (code generation and testing). Fig. 10 shows the transformation scheme of the requirements model into the design model.

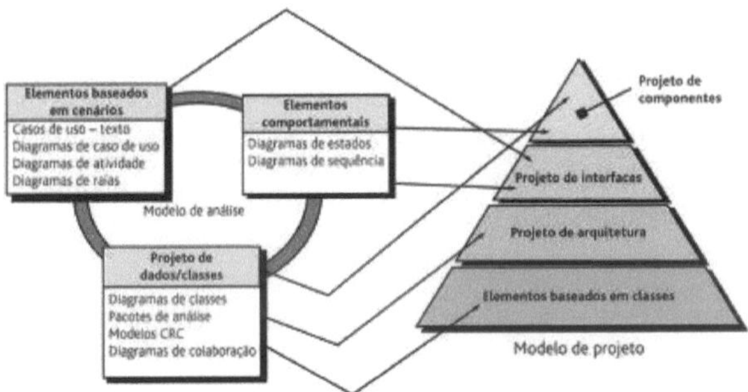

Fig. 10 - Transforming the requirements model into the project model.
Source: Pressman and Maxim (2016, p.226).

Sommerville (2011, p.25) explains that a software project is a description of the software structure to be implemented, the models and data structures used by the system, the interfaces between the system components, sometimes the algorithms used. Pressman and Maxim (2016, p.226) comment that "the requirements model, manifested by scenario-based, class-based, flow-oriented and behavioural elements, feeds into the design task. Thus the project task is made up of the activities of

(1) data/class design;

(2) architectural project;

(3) interface design and;

(4) design of components (Fig. 10).

Sommerville (2011, p.26) apud Schirigatti (2020, p. 114) presents in Fig. 10, the activities of the design process such as: architecture design, interface design, component design and database design, where:

- -The inputs of the design process are: platform information, requirements specification, data description [which are the outputs of the requirements process].
- -The outputs of the design process are: system architecture, database specification, interface specification and component specification.
- -The activities of the project process are: architecture design, interface design and component design, and all converging to the database design.

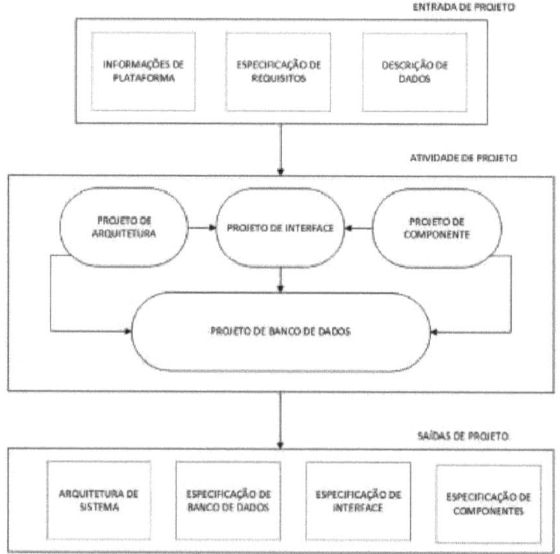

Fig. 11 - Project Process

Source: Sommerville (2011, p.26).

The project activities shown in Fig. 11 are also called the "project model", and according to Pressman and Maxim (2016, p.243), the project model uses several of the UML diagrams used in the analysis model; more implementation-specific details are provided and emphasis is placed on the structure and style of the architecture, the components that reside in that architecture, as well as the interfaces between the components [...].

The **project phase** can be constituted and two main activities:

(1) architectural design and; (2) detailed design.

In the **architecture project** activity the implementation diagrams are developed. Pressman and Maxim (2016, p. 226), the Architecture project: defines the relationships between the main structural elements of software, architectural styles and design patterns, where it is possible to identify the overall structure of the system and its main components. It is where it covers the software elements, their visible properties (attributes) and their relationships.

An example of layers used in architectural design is shown in table 4 below. These layers are used in various layered architecture diagrams, representing the communication between the components through standardised interfaces. Each package is independent and can be organised internally into n-layers.

Table 4 - Layers used in architectural design

Layers	Components
Middleware (software and operating system services)	*Applets* (small programmes that carry out specific activities)
User interface layer	Canvas pack
Layer of business rule	Business rules packages

Layer of persistence	JDBC (set of class and interfaces)
	ODBC (database connection interfaces)
Data	Table and Stored procedures

Note in table (4) that the layers of an architecture project use components such as software services (*Applets*) in the *Middleware layer*, screen packets in the interface layer, business rule packets in the business rule layer, a set of class and connection interfaces in the persistence layer, and tables and Store procedures (data structures and database programming code) in the data layer.

The detailed design is the detailing of the software design composed of (1) interface design, where the interfaces between the system components are defined, and (2) component design are blocks that make up the software architecture and communicate with other systems and entities. Examples of components: executables, libraries, tables, documents, etc. The types of components would be: database, file or data source, documents, static or dynamic library and executable component in a node. Also the detail phase of the project consists of the (3) database design that projects the data structures of the system and how they should be represented in a database. A database design involves (1) requirements analysis, in this case this activity is covered in the software specification phase; (2) logical design, consisting of conceptual data model diagrams that show the data and its relationships, using the DER (entity relationship diagram) or UML (class diagrams).

> "The product of a conceptual project are the sets of Relationship Entity diagrams passed through the stage of analysis of entities and relationships and the elaboration of the RSD diagrams. The RSD product should in fact be the entire structural concept of a database (SCHIRIGATTI, 2020, p. 83)

For Pressman and Maxim (2016, p. 226), "the architectural design defines the relationships between the main structural elements of software, architectural styles and design patterns [...]". For Sommerville (2011, p.25), the architectural design, in which it is possible to identify the overall structure of the system, the main components (sometimes called subsystems or modules), their relationships and how they are distributed. Hirama (2012, p.80), comments that the software architecture is a system structure or structures that comprises the software elements, their externally visible properties (attributes) and their relationships. The architecture is the result of a set of technical and business decisions.

> The project activity aims to establish a software architecture that is achievable. In this activity, some design decisions are made to meet non-functional requirements such as performance, reliability and maintainability. Unlike the analysis, in the project the question to be answered is: "How will the software be developed? The answer is the software architecture represented by an architecture model, which can be a repository-based model, server-client model, cascading model or their combinations. Once a system architecture model has been defined, the next activity is to decompose the system into modules (Hirama, 2012, p.79).

In UML modelling, the elements of a diagram can be grouped in packages, following any grouping criteria. For example, "use cases" can be grouped into packages according to functional business criteria, system components can also be grouped into packages, and each package could be delivered to a different team or programmer (Martins, 2010, p. 163).

The Interface project: Sommerville (2011, p.25) comments that the interface project is where the interfaces between the system components are defined.

Pressman and Maxim (2016, p.226), explains that the interface design communicates with systems that operate together and with the people who use it. An interface implies a flow of information (e.g. data and/or control) and a specific type of behaviour. Behavioural models and usage scenarios used in this model. UML sequence diagrams are used in this model.

The activities in the development cycle of a web application would be:

- Requirements engineering: survey activities and analysis of customer requirements. It generates a context for the use of requirements. Fig.12 shows that it is necessary to perform a Checklist of the client's requirements.

Fig. 12 - Check list of customer requirements
Source: freepik (2020)

- Specifications: generates a graphic representation of the structure (task model) for the next "Website design" activity (Fig.13).

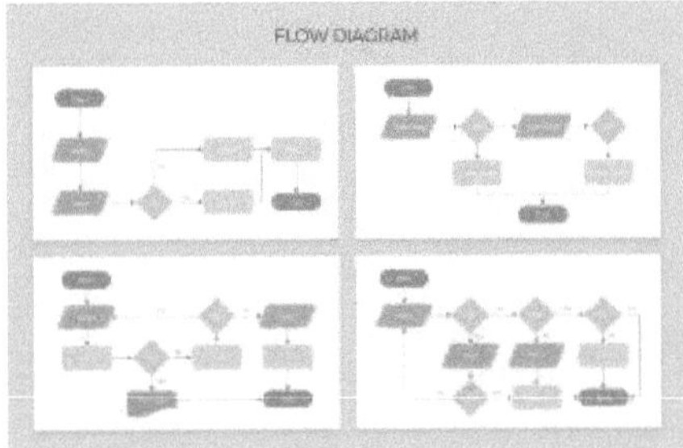

Fig. 13 - Graphic representations
Source: freepik (2020)

- Website design: this generates a data model, graphic design (interfaces) and software architecture for its implementation (coding). The interface design is included in the website design process (Fig.14).

Fig. 14 - Website design
Source: freepik (2020)

- Implementation, use and evaluation of the website: this includes the website for the user's use, possible modifications, metrics for evaluation and new requirements (Fig.15).

Fig. 15 - use and evaluation of the site
Source: freepik / stories (2020)

- Manuals and support: after the implementation, use and evaluation of the web site, manuals and end-user support are generated for the continuity and survival of the software (Fig.16).

Fig. 16 - availability of manuals online
Source: freepik / macrovector_official (2020)

For the development of an interface with effective and efficient usability, several diagrams are used in an interface design. An example of interface representation is through externally visible public operations of a class, as shown in Fig. 17.

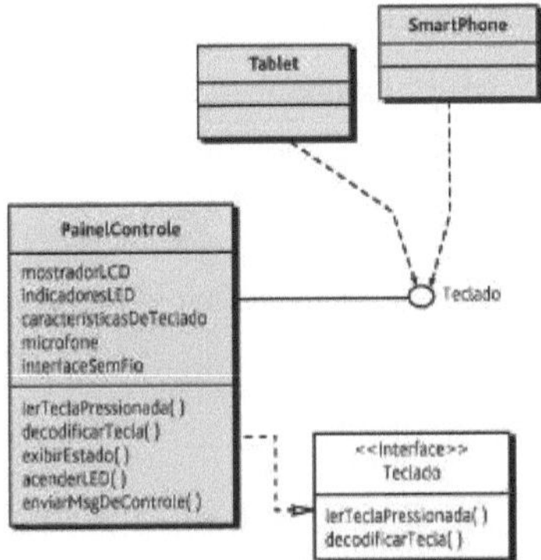

Fig. 17 - Control Panel Interface Representation.
Source: Pressman and Maxim (2016, p.246).

Pressman and Maxim (2016, p.246) comment that the Interface, called keyboard, is presented as a stereotype <<interface>>, [...]. The interface is defined without any attributes and set of operations required to obtain the behaviour of a keyboard.

The component **design**, according to UML, is a modularized part, it is the physical part, which can be deployed and replaced through encapsulation and implementation in a system, and displays a set of interfaces. It can be conceptualized with a realization of interfaces, in other words would be components or blocks that make up the software architecture and communicate with other systems and entities. Examples of components: executables, libraries, tables, documents, etc. The types of components would be: database, file or data source, documents, static or dynamic library and executable component in a node.

For Pressman and Maxim (2016, p. 247), the software component design fully describes the internal details of each software component. To this end, the component level design defines data structures for all local data objects and algorithmic details. The possible UML diagrams that could meet the component design in the design model would be: component diagrams, design classes, activity diagrams and sequence diagrams.

In the database project, Sommerville (2011, p.26) reports that data structures are designed for the system and how they should be represented in a database. A database project involves three steps: requirement analysis, logical design and logical model:

- Requirements analysis: this activity is contemplated with more emphasis in the software specification phase, where the collection and analysis of requirements with the client is carried out. It can be improved at this stage of defining the business rules in the database.

- Logical design: Consisting of conceptual data model diagrams that show the data and its relationships, through the DER (entity relationship diagram) or UML (class diagrams). One of the diagrams most used for data modeling in the conceptual design phase is the DER (Relationship Entity Diagram) as illustrated in Fig. 18.

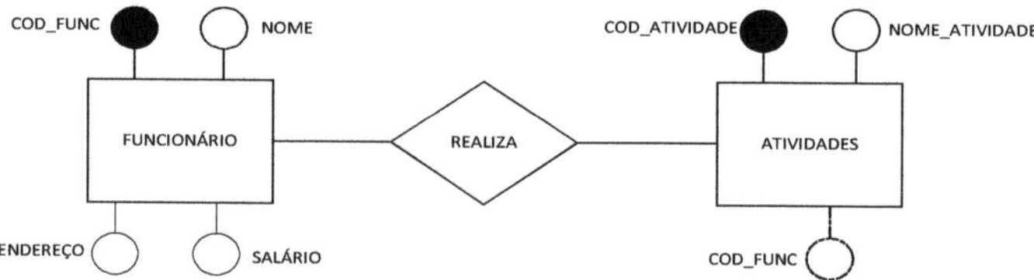

Fig. 18 - Relationship Entity Diagram
Source: Schirigatti (2020, p. 84)

According to Schirigatti (2020, p.84). the rectangles in Fig. 18 represent the entities or collections of objects, the rhombus represents the relationship between the entities, the leaked circles are the simple attributes or properties of the entities, the completed attributes are the primary keys (PK) and the dashed attribute is the foreign key that effects the relationship between the entities.

The product of a conceptual project are the sets of Relationship Entity diagrams, passed through the stage of analysis of entities, attributes and relationships, and the elaboration of the RSD diagrams. Fig. 19 presents a diagram referring to the stages of the database project, which lies between the requirements gathering and analysis activities and the Logical and Physical project activities.

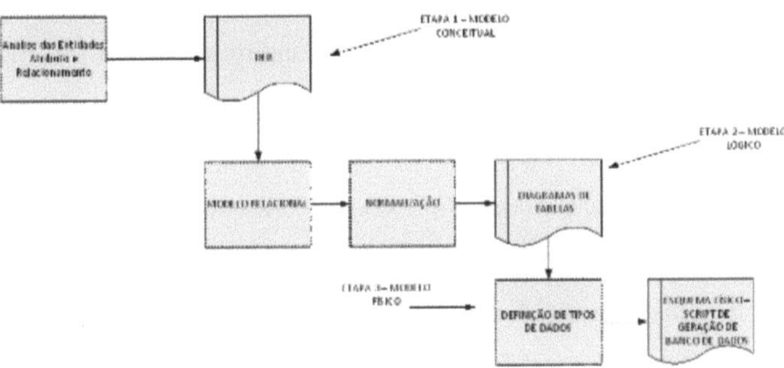

Fig. 19 - Stages before and after the RSD diagram
Source: Schirigatti (2020, p. 92)

The RSD product must in fact be the entire structural concept of a Database. After completion of the DER Stage, the logical modelling stage is carried out, initiated by Relational Mapping.

A database project also involves a logical, abstraction-level model seen by the DBMS (Database Management Systems) user. The logical model describes a structure that does not affect the structure of a Database, but can affect the performance of applications. Within the logical model is the relational model, this is the case of the representation in the example below, given the relationship between the Employee and Activity table: The underlined fields are primary and relationship keys

Official = (<u>Cod func</u>, Name, Address, Salary)
Activity = (<u>Cod activity, Cod func, Activity name</u>)

For Schirigatti (2020, p.93)

> "In the logical database modeling stage for software production, standardization procedures are essential to avoid redundancy and imperfections in relationships between entities. After the standardization procedures the appropriate table diagrams are performed".

In a database project the standardization process is a step in the logical modeling that consists of a series of checks applied to a given table. With these checks it is possible to certify that certain conditions are met (SCHIRIGATTI, 2020, p. 93). In this sense, the standardisation process exists independently of any type of information representation, but it has developed with the advent of the relational database model. This model represents the classes of entities and their relationships by means of tables and relationships (FERRAZ, 2003, p.153). The main normal forms are the first normal form (1FN), second normal form (2FN), third normal form (3FN) and Boyce-Codd normal form (FNBC) which is also called the fourth normal form. These forms have increasingly restrictive requirements, [we will see that] every relation in FNBC is also in 3FN, and every relation in 3FN is in 2FN and every relation in 2FN is in 1FN (SCHIRIGATTI, 2020, p. 94) apud (RAMAKRISHNAN AND GEHRKE, 2011, p.19).

The diagram in Fig. 19 in understandable form for the generation of tables and fields for the database, closest to the understanding of the DBMS. In Fig. 20, Mannino (2008, p.157) shows the class diagram that contains classes (groups of objects), associations (binary relationships) between classes and characteristics of objects (attributes and operations).

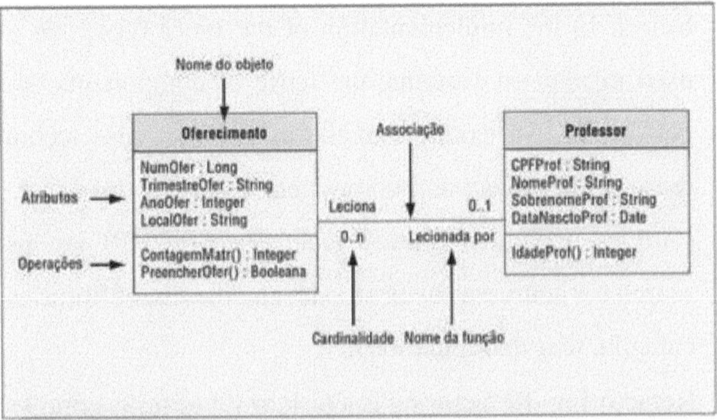

Fig. 20 - Stages before and after the RSD diagram

Source: Mannino (2008, p. 153)

The class diagram supports object-oriented modeling by providing an alternative to RSD ratings. Now let's look at the next step in the software development process, called the software implementation step.

2.1.3 Software implementation step

After the project phase, the software implementation phase begins, i.e. this phase is related to the development of the programming/encoding of the software. According to Sommerville (2011, p.135-136) the most critical stage of the software development process is the implementation of the system, the stage where the software executable is created. Implementation involves the development of high or low level programming languages, customizations and adaptations of purchased ready-made systems that meet specific requirements of a company.

There are several programming techniques, the three main ones are (1) reuse, (2) refactoring, (3) configuration management and (4) host-target development, where they can be used in a hybrid way:

- Reuse: In the implementation of the reuse type, one of the most used in modern systems, the reuse of components or systems is performed. An example of the use of the reuse technique is the reuse at the object and component level. At this level, validation routines or functionalities such as CPF/CNPJ are used, in the search for addresses by postcode, and the use of libraries (graphics, calicula, text manipulation).

- Refactoring: Refactoring is a task or set of tasks complementary to the software development process and is specifically applied at the coding and implementation stage. Refactoring aims at simplifying and optimizing the code, achieving significant improvements in the coding process and, consequently, in the software development project with deliverable and in the construction process. The refactoring technique makes changes, modifications and simplifications to the internal structure, but its external behaviour remains unchanged. It is widely used and combined with the agile software methodologies, specifically XP, which considerably stimulates refactoring. However, refactoring can cause certain side effects and it is necessary to use appropriate tools and tests to verify that the external behaviour has not been changed.

Refactoring is a reorganization technique that simplifies the design (or code) of a component without changing its function or behavior. Thus, "refactoring is the process of changing a software system in such a way that it does not change the external behaviour of the [design] code, although it improves its internal structure" (PRESSMAN, 2016, p.238). Therefore, refactoring is a basic technique for code improvement. Feathers (2013, p. 389), in his book Effective work with legacy code, explains an essential method of refactoring: the extraction method. Through it, it is possible to systematically divide large existing methods into smaller ones, i.e. code that is easier to understand, reusing and avoiding duplicating the logic in other areas of the system. For Kerievsky (2008, p. 34), refactoring is a transformation that preserves behaviour and can be considered a change in the internal structure or codification of the software for a better understanding, being less costly to modify and without changes in its observable behaviour. Refactoring is a process that involves the removal of duplication, simplification of conditional logic and clarification of code that is unclear. In this sense, refactoring is an optimization process that must be safely performed from manual and automated tests. The premise of the refactoring technique is to perform the process in small steps or steps, which helps to prevent the insertion of defects in the code. According to Kerievsky (2008, p. 37), the refactoring technique justifies its use:

a) improve the existing code design: it constantly involves searching for code problems and immediate removal when found;

b) getting a better understanding of the code: improving the code is not just about commenting on it, but is clearly understandable;

c) making programming less annoying: it means better structure the coding, separating it into smaller classes for a better understanding, understanding and integration of code.

However, refactoring always tends to break out of a pattern due to continuous adjustments and improvements in the project. However, with the recommended reading of Refactoring for

Patterns, you will see that author Joshua Kerievsky comments that it is possible to refactor towards a pattern in the code.

- Configuration Management: in the configuration management technique, Sommerville (2011, p.136) comments that it is the practice of versioning and managing the various different versions of software components.

- Host-target Technique: in Host-target Technique performing the development work is performed on a computer (host) or development platform and executed on another computer called target.

2.1.4 Software validation (testing) stage

After the software implementation step the next step is testing. For Sommerville (2011, p.146) "the test is intended to show that a program does what it is proposed to do and to discover the defects of the program before use. When testing the software, the program is run using fictitious data". According to Sommerville (2011, p.146) the testing process has two objectives: (1) to demonstrate that the requirements have been met and (2) to find out whether the software has anomalies, errors or is behaving incorrectly.

The important thing about the testing process is that it should not only be considered an inspection at the final stage of the software development process, but should be performed at all stages of the process. There should be testing processes when designing, preparing the data, running the program and the inspection tests.

2.1.5 Software evolution stage

In the last phase of the software development process the "evolution" is considered the software update activities concerning future improvements for the survival of the software life cycle. In this case the software evolution occurs through software updates due to new internal and external business rules and updates of technical or legislative government standards and specifications.

2.2 Traditional software development models

The software processes are aimed at (traditional) plans or agile processes. In this topic we will understand what are the main models of the traditional (classic) software development process.

One of the first software development models, the cascade model, was first exposed in 1970, being of iterative activities [where they pass through several versions], but not incremental, [i.e. constituted part by part] (SCHACH, 2010, p.42).

2.2.1 Cascade Model

As one of the first software development models, it serves primary stages of the software development process. According to Sommerville (2011, p.19) the cascade model considers the fundamental activities of the specification process, development, validation and evolution, [sequential and systematic] and represents each of the distinct phases such as: requirements specification, software design, implementation, testing and so on. Sometimes called the classical life cycle, as illustrated in Fig. 21 the cascade model. For Pressman (2016, p.42), the cascade model is the oldest model of Software Engineering, and its effectiveness is questionable, such problems are reported as: (1) actual projects do not follow the sequential flow proposed by the model; (2) the cascade model requires the client to establish all needs at the beginning of the project; (3) versions are not available during the project.

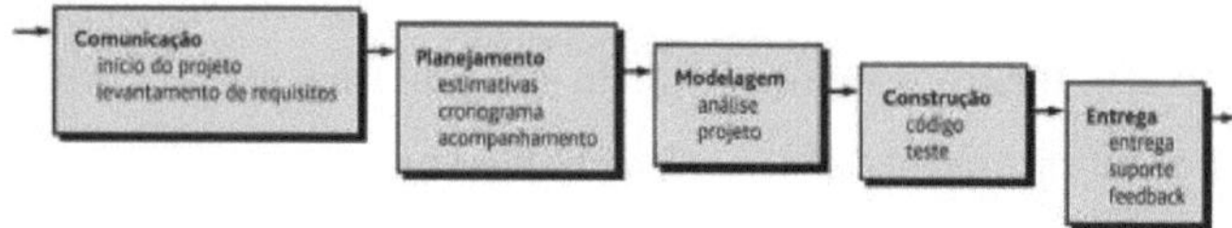

Fig. 21 - Cascade model
Source: Pressman (2016, p.142)

A critical point regarding the cascade model is that no phase is completed until the documentation for that phase has been completed and the products of that phase have been approved by the SQA (software quality assurance) group. This entails changes (SCHACH, 2010, p.51), i.e. as shown in Fig. 22, if there are changes, the process will only continue if the changes to the documents are carried out and checked by SQA.

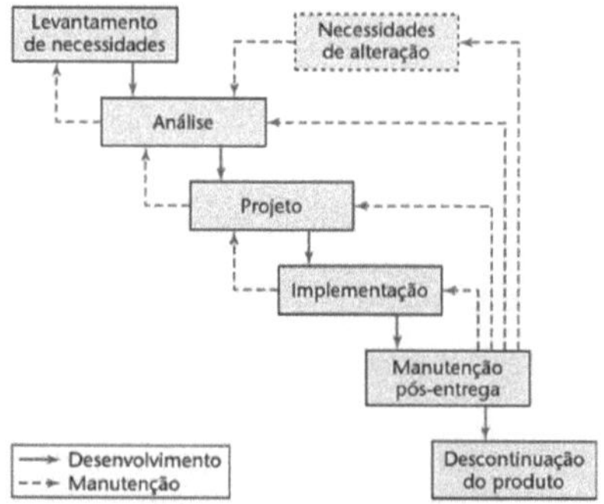

Fig. 22 - The full cascade life cycle model
Source: Schach (2010, p. 51)

In the cascade paradigm a test stage is not formed as it presents a life cycle of a software development methodology. In this model, all stages perform the tests and the return of the due adjustments, as a maintenance cycle, continuous throughout the software development process, however, presents an evolutionary phase of maintenance after software delivery, providing a maintenance feedback. For Pressman (2016, p.43), today the work with software is very fast and subject to a chain of endless changes (in features, functions and information content). The cascade model is often inadequate for such work.

Lessa and Lessa Junior. (2009, p.2), comment on the advantages of cascading development, is that "it allows departmental and managerial control. A planning can be assigned a deadline for each stage of development and a product can proceed in the development process, theoretically and be delivered on time [...]". The disadvantage of Lessa and Lessa Junior (2009, p.2) is that it does not allow much flexibility or revision. The first time an application is in the testing stage it is very difficult to return and change something that was not very heavy on the conceptual stage.

2.2.2 Incremental Model

The Incremental model, also called the Interaction model, according to Schach (2010, p.41) uses an iterative and incremental life model, as shown in Fig. 23, which presents the development of a software product and four increments called increments A, increment B, increment C and increment D. The horizontal axis is the time axis, and the vertical one refers to man-hour.

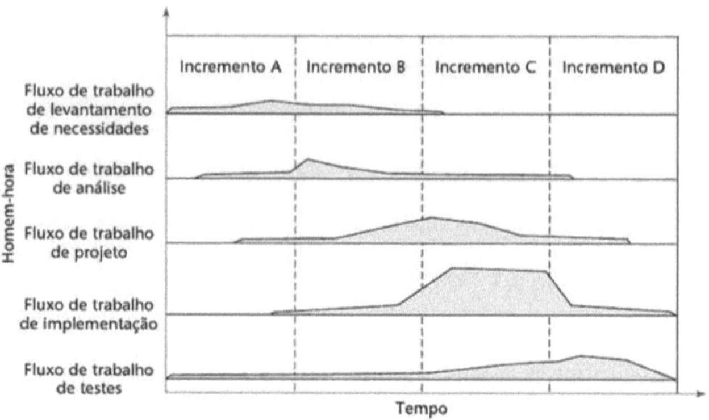

Fig. 23 - Construction of a software product in four increments
Source: Schach (2010, p.43)

For Pressman (2016, p.44), "the incremental model combines linear [cascade model] and parallel process flows of the elements [...]".

Figures 22 and 23 show that the incremental model applies linear sequences (workflows) in a staggered manner as time moves forward (time axis). Each linear sequence produces software deliverable "increments". Fig. 23, on the vertical axis, shows the application of workflows over time (horizontal axis). Fig. 24, on the vertical axis, shows the application of functionalities and features of the software and on the horizontal axis deals with the project schedule. Each increment is composed of the cascade model (communication, planning, modeling, construction and availability). According to Sommerville (2011, p.31), in an incremental delivery process, customers identify the services to be provided by the system (functional requirements). A series of delivery increments are defined (increment 1, 2, ..., n), with each increment providing a set of functionalities of the system over time. In this way, the incremental model provides quality to the software process, as the customer will gradually receive the system's functionality. Contrary to the cascade model, where the customer or user will have to wait and use the software product, only when the whole system is finished.

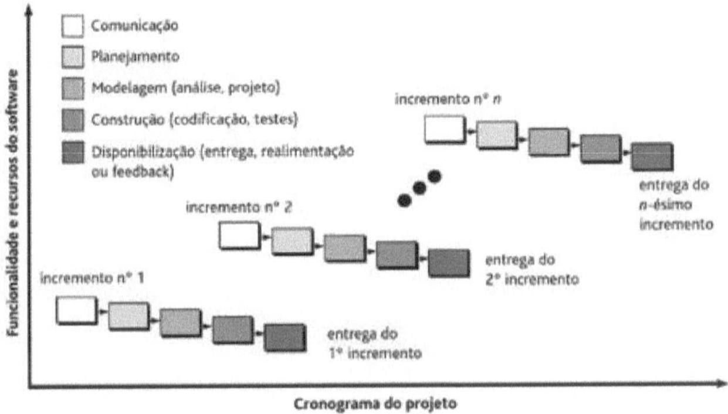

Fig. 24 - Incremental Model
Source: Pressman (2016, p.44)

The use of this model should be avoided for critical systems that involve work teams in different locations, because it is characteristic of the incremental paradigm, the iteration between those involved in the software development team.

For Sommerville (2011, p.32) some advantages of the incremental paradigm would be:

- Customers can use the initial increments as prototypes and gain experience, forming the requirements for the next increments.
- There is no need for re-learning when the system is complete.
- Customers do not have to wait until the whole system is delivered to get from it. The initial increments meet the most critical requirements.

- Customers are less likely to find software failures in the most important parts, as prioritised increments receive a greater amount of testing.

For Sommerville (2011, p.32) some disadvantages of the incremental paradigm would be:

- Difficulty in identifying common resources needed for all increments, as the requirements are not defined in detail at the beginning of the project, but are defined throughout the project.
- Difficulty in obtaining the functionalities in system changes. In the iterative process there are difficulties in obtaining feedback from the customer regarding functionalities of the old system.
- As in the incremental model there are no complete system specifications at the beginning of the project, this results in difficulties in setting up the system development contract.

2.2.3 Prototyping Model

A prototype is a set of initial or essential features of a low cost product or software and can be a minimum viable product. For Sommerville (2011, p.30) a prototype is one:

> "initial version of a software system, used to demonstrate concepts, experiment design options to discover about the problem and its possible solutions. The rapid and iterative development of the prototype is essential to keep costs under control".

The prototyping model is ideal when the client only defines a few objectives, without detailing the functional requirements or when the developer. Pressman (2016, p. 45) comments that "the prototyping paradigm, regardless of how it is applied [to any software process], when requirements are unclear, [...]

helps those involved to better understand what is being built". feels insecure about the efficiency of any algorithm.

Fig. 25 illustrates the software development cycle in the prototyping model, which begins with communication, holds a meeting with those involved defining the general objectives of the software, identifies the already known requirements and schematizes which areas need a broader definition and after and performs a prototyping iteration, where the prototype is planned through a rapid design modeling. This prototype is delivered and evaluated by those involved where feedback is generated to refine the requirements.

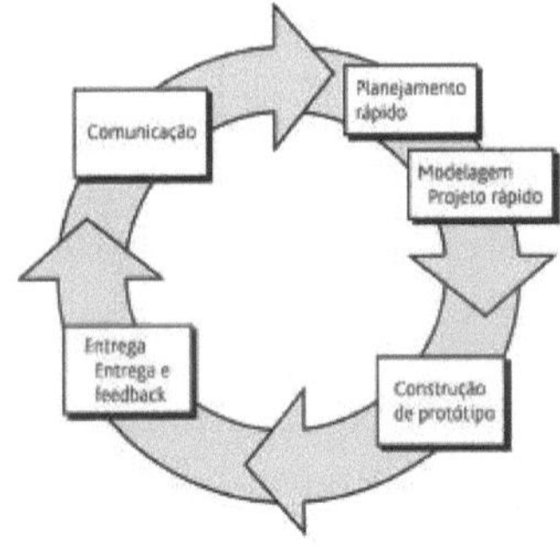

Fig. 25 - Prototyping model
Source: Pressman (2016, p.45)

Modelling by prototyping is more related to the identification of the software requirements, as its characteristic is to support the elicitation and validation of system requirements. Other authors also call this model "rapid prototyping", and operational. Schach (2010, p.320) comments, for example, if the desired product should deal with financial functionalities, then the rapid prototype consists of a product that performs on-screen data capture and prints reports, but does not perform any file updating or error handling. Sommerville (2011, p.30), comments that "a prototype can also get new ideas for the requirements and find strengths and weaknesses of the software, [...] as well as reveal errors and omissions from the proposed requirements".

Some advantages of prototyping would be given by Pressman (2016, P.46); Sommerville (2011, p.32); Schach (2010, p.62) and Audy and Priklandnicki (2008, p.17):

- To define the requirements the prototype is efficient for the software development project, after the specification phase must be discarded.
- In the system design process, a prototype can be used to study specific software solutions.
- Prototypes can be used effectively to provide information on certain categories of risk: such as construction time constraints, verification of the possibility of large-scale software construction by the development team.
- Allows the user to interact more actively in system modeling.
- Facilitates the identification of software requirements.

Possible disadvantages are already given by Pressman (2016, P.46); Sommerville (2011, p.32); Schach (2010, p.62) and Audy and Priklandnicki (2008, p.17):

- It may be impossible to adjust the prototype to meet non-functional requirements such as performance, protection, robustness and reliability.
- If there is pressure to turn a prototype into a product, the quality will be compromised.

- The client wants results and often does not know, or does not understand that a prototype can be far from ideal software, which he does not even imagine what it is like. Even so, the manager often gives in to complaints and tries to shorten the delivery time, which was already properly planned.

2.2.4 Boehm Spiral Model

"The spiral model is an evolutionary software process model that unites the iterative nature of prototyping with the systematic and controlled aspects of the cascade model" (PRESSMAN, 2016, p.47). Note that modeling goes through its engineering evolution, through transformations, a combination of models, which become hybrid models. Sommerville (2011, p.32) comments that the spiral model is a risk-oriented framework, was proposed by Boehm (1988), where the software process is represented by a spiral and not as a sequence of activities with some returns from one to another. Audy and Priklandnicki (2008, p.15), comment that the spiral model, also called "spiral life cycle" or "Boehm's paradigm", contains a new element in its process, "risk analysis".

The Boehm Spiral model has four important activities reported by Audy and Priklandnicki (2008, p.15):

- Planning: determining objectives.
- Risk analysis: analysis of alternatives and identification/resolution of risks.
- Engineering: product development.
- Customer Evaluation: evaluation of engineering results.

Fig. 26 shows the Boehm software process spiral model, where each turn of the spiral is divided into four sectors: goal setting (alternatives and constraints), risk assessment and reduction (risk identification and resolution - HR - risk analysis), development and assessment and planning (planning next phases of the cycle).

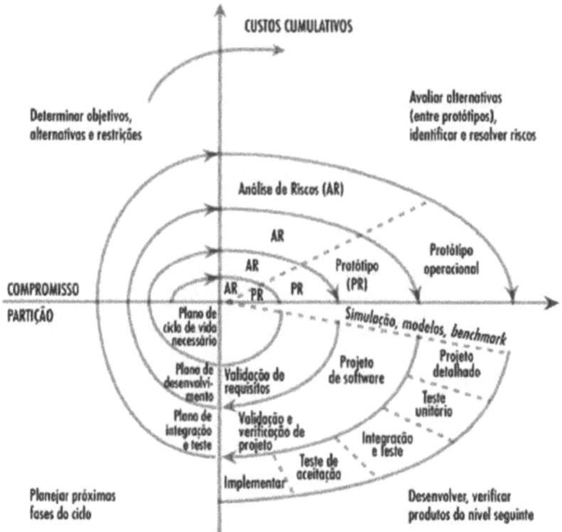

Fig. 26 - Boehm model

Source: Audy and Priklandnicki (2008, p.18)

Some advantages of spiral modelling are given by Pressman (2016, P.46), Sommerville (2011, p.32), Schach (2010, p.62) and Audy and Priklandnicki (2008, p.17):

- Explicit recognition of risk, i.e. risk management is a very important activity of the project and is one of the essential parts of project management.
- It uses prototyping to reduce risks before they become problematic.
- Prevention and change to tolerances.
- Model used for internal projects in companies (large scale production), because if the identification of risks is noticeable and

the project is cancelled, the project team can be reallocated to the functional aeras.

- Assumption that the software will be developed in discrete phases, which in fact the process is interactive and incremental.

Some disadvantages of spiral modelling are given by Pressman (2016, P.46); Sommerville (2011, p.32), Schach (2010, p.62) and Audy and Priklandnicki (2008, p.17):

- No use of the model for external developers, because if the risks are detected, there will be a breach of contract.

- Restriction on project size is applied to large-scale software development projects and prescriptive documentation, as there is a high cost for conducting risk analysis.

- The team must have risk analysis skills, as it is possible that the team may believe that the project is going well, which may be a mistake, and the project is heading for the precipice.

2.2.5 RUP Model - Rational Unified Process

The RUP (Rational Unified Process) is a hybrid model that uses UML standards and unifies the software development process using various resources from other models, both traditional and agile models. Thus it can be said that the RIP is "an attempt to take advantage of the best resources and characteristics of traditional software process models, but characterising them in such a way as to implement many of the best principles of agile software development" Pressman (2016, p.56-57). "It is IBM's proprietary process, which provides techniques for software development with the aim of increasing performance and productivity. RUP uses objective guidelines and UML to illustrate actions" (NEVES, 2014, p.51). The RUP model is an example of a modern process model or hybrid software development model, derived from work on UML and the associated *Unifield Software Development Process*. (RUNBAUGH, et. al., 1999; ARLOW and NEUSTADT, 2005) apud Sommerville (2011, p.34).

For Martins (2010, p.170),

> The OR model, is a simplification of reality that describes the system from a certain point of view, and works with UML models: (1) analysis model, (2) database model, (3) use case model, (4) deployment model, (5) implementation model, (6) business model, (7) design model and (8) test model.

Fig. 27 shows a diagram of the steps of the OR model:

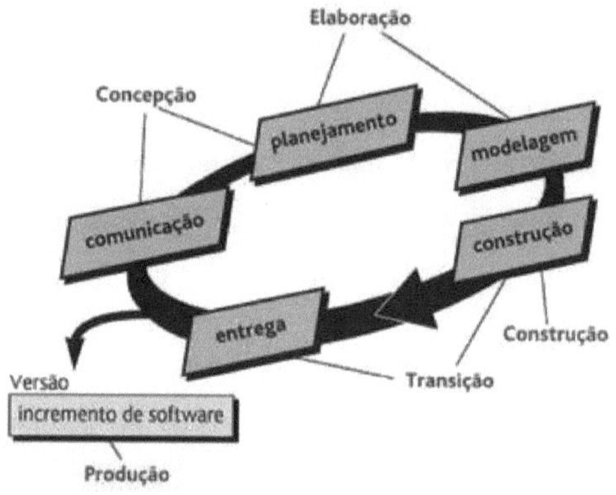

Fig. 27 - RUP model - IBM refined process
Source: Pressman (2016, p.57)

Pressman (2016, p.57) shows in Fig. 26 that the OMR model, includes the design activities (communication with clients and planning), the elaboration phase includes the planning and modeling activities of the generic process. It also includes the construction phase, where I develop and purchase software components. The transition phase covers the last stages of construction activity and the first delivery or delivery versions. And finally the production phase, which would be the sum of all the software increments that confer the product to the customer.

The OR model is based on 4Ps: People, Project, Product and Process, and is based on five pillars: requirements management, componentised architecture, software quality assessment and software change management (NEVES, 2014, p.51). The OR model also consists of perspectives, such as static, practical and dynamic. Let's see each one of them:

    a) Static Perspective: Martins (2010, p.170) comments on the static structure, where the processes of the OR define roles, activities, artifacts worked and the procedures that must be performed. The processes define "who" is executing "what" and "when". The static workflows in the RUP (tasks of the software process), are the:

- Business Modeling: modeled through business use cases;
- Requirements: actors interacting with the system are identified and use cases are developed to model the system requirements;
- Analysis and design: the project model is created and documented with architectural models, component models, object models and sequence models,
- Implementation: System components are implemented and structured in implementation subsystems. Automatic code generation from project templates helps accelerate these processes, testing, implementation, configuration and change management and environment.
- Testing: testing is an iterative process that is done in conjunction with implementation. The system test follows the completion of the implementation.

- Deployment: a product release is created, distributed to users and installed at their workplace.

- Configuration and Change Management: This support workflow manages system changes.

- Project Management: support workflow that manages the development of the system.

- Environment: workflow related to the provision of appropriate tools for the software development team.

b) Practical Perspective: Under the practical perspective of the OMR, good software engineering practices recommended for software development are suggested: "i. develop software iteratively, ii. manage requirements, iii. use component based architectures, iv. model software virtually, v. check software quality and vi. control software changes" SOMMERVILLE (2011, p.35).

c) Dynamic perspective: the perspective is related to the order in which the activities should be carried out (phases). Static and dynamic perspectives are confused, they are seen in a unique way (Hirama, 2012, p.42).

Fig. 28, according to Hirama (2012, p.40), shows the unified process, the phases of the process (design, drafting, construction and transition) and the main workflows (requirements, analysis and design, implementation and testing), according to the static perspective (workflows).

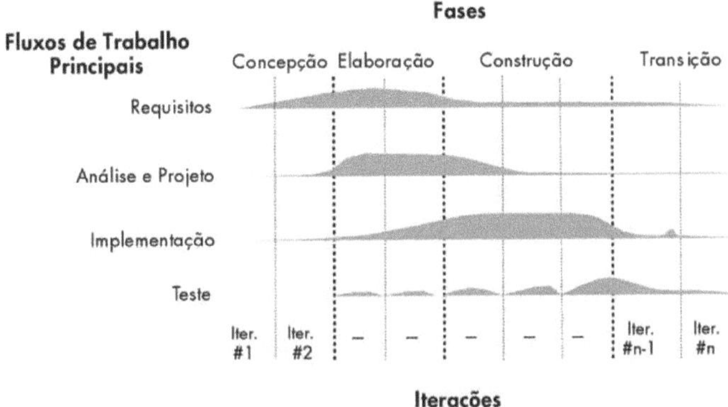

Fig. 28 - RUP model - IBM refined process
Source: Pressman (2016, p.57)

As OR is an iterative development approach, it provides software in an incremental way, that is, it has a dynamic perspective. It is possible to see in Fig. 27 the various iterations (1 to n iterations) for the software development workflows. We can cite some advantages given by Pressman (2016, P.46), Sommerville (2011, p.32), Schach (2010, p.62) and Audy and Priklandnicki (2008, p.17):

- It is an approach that potentially combines the three generic process models: cascade, incremental and reuse.
- It separates the workflows phases and recognition that software deployment in a user environment is part of the process.
- Phases are defined by goals and not by activities. The iterations have deadlines defined within the phases. In other words, the phases are dynamic.

- Workflows are static and are technical activities that are not associated with a phase, but can be used throughout the development to achieve the goals.

- It is an object-oriented approach. It uses UML modeling to illustrate the actions.

- In the "design" phase (communication and modelling) (Fig. 27), the basis of the architecture is not a prototype, as it is not disposable. In some cases, the elaboration generates an "executable architecture base".

- Created to overcome difficulties imposed by the cascade model.

- It considers that each increment is built from previous results, updating and correcting previous deliveries.

- Uses the code already developed to increase productivity and optimize resources.

Some disadvantages of OR modelling are given by Pressman (2016, P.46); Sommerville (2011, p.32), Schach (2010, p.62) and Audy and Priklandnicki (2008, p.17):

- It is not a suitable process for all types of development, such as embedded software development.

- It takes time to show results to the client, and can cause impatience and lack of confidence.

- Difficulty to go back to earlier phases when problems are detected in the current phase, with greater cost related to the implementation of the necessary adjustments.

- Likelihood of disappointment on the part of the user upon receiving the final problem.

- Cost related to the accommodation of project changes.
- The development team is always almost finished, being asked about the progress of the process.
- It covers the risks for a long time.
- Delays the solution of critical risks.

We have seen that software development models are activities that produce a better definition, modeling, construction and quality of software construction. We can work with these activities in order to better plan and control the scope, time and cost resources. This form is called a project management approach. To better understand the project management of software development and modeling and/or database implementation, we must understand how project management should act in the company's areas.

2.3 Agile software development methodologies

The agile software methodology is the performance of requirements gathering, planning, design, implementation and testing activities, of fast manufacturing, through a series of feature enhancements, short time interactions and customer approved deliveries. The software is not developed as a single unit, but as a series of increments each increment includes new system functionality. Agile software development methods use faster and more objective systematisation to produce software. The agile software development process is characterized by the speed of manufacturing useful software, reducing bureaucracy through few artifacts (documents). Through iterations of execution of activities in short spaces of time (maximum of one month), where it is possible to make alterations with the client reducing the risks of the project, thus becoming a "light" project. Another familiar feature of the agile development process is the focus on priorities and the use of agile prototypes and models, thus becoming a light project.

Software engineering and software development methodologies were inspired by manufacturing processes to consolidate their working methods. Born in the second half of the 20th century through theories and production methods (Fordism and Taylorism) (PRIKLANDNICKI, MILLANI, 2014, p.16).

In the 1980s and early 1990s, there was a widespread view that the best way to achieve the best software was through careful project planning, formalized security quality, the use of analysis and design methods supported by CASE (*Computer-aided-software engineering*) tools, and the rigorous and controlled software development process (SOMMERVILLE, 2011, p.39).

This perception was applied to the development of large corporate systems, such as government, aerospace and large corporate systems, through a heavy and plan-driven development approach, with large teams, geographically dispersed and long development periods. Today, companies work in fast moving, global, interactive, innovative and employee-value environments, i.e., they operate through "agile thinking".

By the mid-1990s, new software development processes were emerging, called "light processes", in response to traditional, slow and bureaucratic methodologies. Let's see below what these agile software development processes are.

2.3.1 Extreme Programming

Currently there are several methodologies of agile software development, such as XP, *Extreme programming (XP)*. According to Baltzan (2016, p. 282), the XP method is one of the widely used methods due to "response to business acceleration, rapid application development has become a popular route to accelerate system development.

The agile software development process is characterized by the speed of manufacturing useful software, reducing bureaucracy through a few artifacts (documents). Through iterations of execution of activities in short spaces of time (maximum of one month), where it is possible to make changes with the client reducing the risks of the project, thus becoming a "light" project. Another familiar feature of the agile development process is the focus on priorities and the use of agile prototypes and models, thus becoming a light project.

Pressman (2016, p.72), comments that *Extreme Programming* employs an object-oriented methodology as its development paradigm and involves a set of constant rules and practices in the context of four activities: planning, design, coding and testing. Fig. 29 shows the *Extreme Programming* (XP) process. Starting with user stories (user requirements), simple design, point solutions (prototypes), coding (pair programming) and unit acceptance testing, a version is then created and delivered.

Fig. 29 - *Extreme Programming* Process
Source: Hirama (2016, p. 45)

For Fagundes (2005, p. 27), in the XP process, where it presents the activity flow of the exploration phases (requirements gathering through user stories), version planning (task cards, estimates, discussion, prioritisation and cost sizing), version plan, codification (production) and iterations for delivery, and project end. This process can be summarised in table 5 below:

Table 5 - steps in the XP software development process.

Summary table of the steps and activities of the agile XP methodology.	
Stage	**Activities**
Requirements	1. Listen to user stories and understand the business environment. 2. Development of Story Cards (user cards).
Version planning	1. Task Cards. 2. Estimates of the effort of each task. 3. Discussion and prioritisation. 4. Cost dimensioning.
Project	1. CRC cards (employee class). Object oriented class organization.
Coding - iterations	1. Stories implemented (through pair programming - two people working together) and refactoring.
Tests	2. Acceptance tests. 3. Customer approval. 4. Availability to the client.

The agile practices of extreme programming can be specified as follows: (1) cohesive team; (2) user stories; (3) short circuits; (4) acceptance testing; (5) pair programming; (6) continuous integration; (7) sustainable pace; (8) open work area; (9) simple project; (10) refactoring.

However, the XP method, has an emphasis on programming/encoding (Fig. 30), as the peer programme: [...] the code is written by pairs of programmers working together on the same workstation. One member of each pair commands the keyboard and enters the code. The other member of the pair observes the code being typed, looking for errors and improvements. The two interact intensely" (MARTIN and MARTIN, 2011, p. 41).

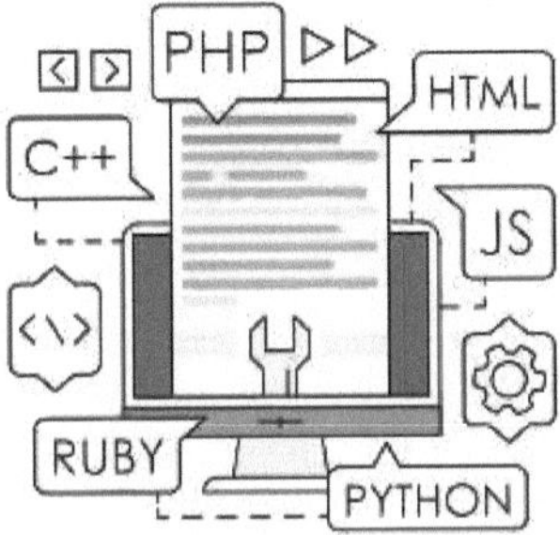

Fig. 30 - Scrum features

Source: freepik / artmonkey (2020)

In short, extreme programming, like any other agile method, divides a project into small steps, where developers cannot move on to the next phase until the previous one is completed. Emphasizing that the faster the communication and returns among the team, the better the results will be.

2.3.2 *Scrum* - fast software management

Scrum is a fast software management methodology, and can be combined with software development methodologies. It has an interactive approach, where the analysis starts as soon as some requirements are available, and then design and coding activities begin, working with small parts at a time, which are tested, approved and delivered to the client. Fig. 31 illustrates features of the Scrum method: (1) teamwork; (2) agile methodology; (3) working with Sprints (revisions); (4) planning.

Fig. 31 - Scrum features

Source: freepik / macrovector_official (2020)

Pressman (2016, p.78) comments that *Scrum* is an agile software development methodology designed by Jeff Sutherland and his development team in the early 1990s. Fig. 32 shows the flow of the Scrum process.

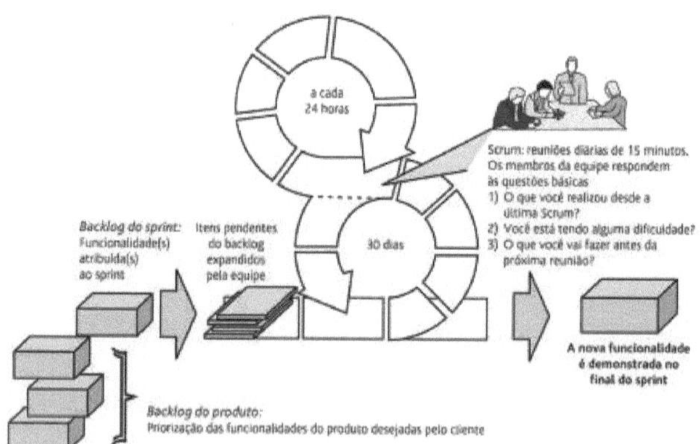

Fig. 32 - Scrum process

Source: Pressman (2016, p. 45)

Scrum can also be used for any other type of product, not necessarily software. It has an interactive approach, where the analysis starts as soon as some requirements are available, and then design and coding activities start, working with small parts at a time, which are tested, approved and delivered to the customer.

The agility ceremonies, within a software development process or product of Scrum methodology, according to Massari (2018), has five ceremonies, all with limited time (*Timeboxed*):

1. *Sprint*: which is a time-limited interaction that can last from two weeks to one month, generating a launchable product for the customer or market. During the execution of the interaction, the sprint will not be able to suffer alterations that compromise the determined goal. It is also considered the period that the team has to execute what was defined in the initial meeting. Sommerville (2011, p.50) *Sprint* is a planning unit in which the work to be done is evaluated, the resources for development are selected and the software is implemented. At the end of *Sprint*, the complete functionality is delivered.

2. Sprint *Planning* Meeting: held on the first day of a sprint, a ceremony also called Inception. For Massari and Vidal (2018, p.100) "The aim of the Inception phase is to develop and plan the MVP (MVP - *Minimum Variable Product*)". The planned MVP is transformed into the Product Backlog, which is the main output of Inception. According to Massari (2018), it is defined what will be done and how it will be done. The *Product Owner,* who defines and prioritizes the project items, elaborates a vision of the product, presenting it.

3. *Daily Scrum*: is a 15 minute daily meeting, where the development team shares knowledge, answering 3 questions: what I did yesterday, what I will do today, and what are the impediments. Still in the *Daily* Scrum ceremony, the *Scrum Master* (Team Leader), guarantees the execution of the meetings and the Timeboxed to be followed.

4. *Sprint Review*, is the ceremony held at the end of Sprint to inspect the MVP generated product increment, being the simplest version of a product. The development team presents the results and the Owner Product approves or not the delivery.

5. *Retrospective* of the *Sprint*, is another ceremony held at the end of the sprint. This ceremony is held to reflect on possible improvements to the project.

According to Martins (2007, p. 269),

> Scrum is a very light process to manage and control software development projects and product creation. *Scrum* is an agile methodology that follows the interactive and incremental philosophies. It focuses on what is really important: managing the project and creating a product that adds value to the business. The value comes from the functionality itself, the time it is needed, the cost and the quality.

Orth and Priklandnicki (2009, p.152), comment that *Scrum* takes an empirical approach, accepting that the problem may not be fully understood or defined in the analysis and that requirements are likely to change over time, focusing on maximizing the team's ability to respond quickly to challenges. The following is table x, where you will find the characteristics of *Scrum's* agile process:

Table 6 - Features of the agile Scrum process.

Features of the agile *Scrum* process

Features	Why?
Fast project management and control	It uses the *Sprint* cycle, where it has a fixed term already closed. The sprint cycle has evaluation, selection, development and review phases. It works with sequential objectives.
Light process	Works with small teams, prioritizes projects. Nothing is generated or applied that will not be effectively useful and used.
Add value to business	Value stems from functionality, timeliness, cost and quality.
Increases communication and maximises cooperation	Works with small teams. Often to demonstrate everything that has been done for the team and for the client.
Prototyping	The work is often focused on a demonstrable product.
Increases quality	In the sprint the revision stage should always be used (inspection and adaptation).
Framework	It provides a working structure, but is not useful if applied alone. It needs to be combined with other methodologies or practices to add value.
Assists the development of complex adaptive products/systems - complex contexts	*Scrum* was created in the context to realize management based on complex adaptive systems theories.
It does not operate in chaotic contexts.	Scrum operates with well defined and stable objectives. Chaotic contexts have objectives that change constantly.
Works in an empirical way	It works with constant feedback in successive cycles. Checking what has been agreed and done, modifying and adapting.
It is based on visibility, inspection and adaptation.	It works on continuous incremental product improvement as well as development processes.

Iterative and incremental.	The product is developed in successive cycles or iterations. In each of these cycles an increment is generated in the product, which is added to and modified what is already ready in the product so far (sprints).
The vision becomes clearer as the process progresses	The Scrum project begins with a vision, which may be vague at first, and then becomes clearer as the project evolves. From the vision is defined a list of prioritized items, composed of requirements and functionalities that need to be built in order for the vision to be realized.

For Pires (2016, p.21) the *Scrum* rapid management process is a similar method to XP, "as small teams, unstable requirements and short iterations to promote visibility for development. However the dimensions in Scrum differ from XP" (SOARES, 2016, p.5), but with a greater focus on management. The management process described by *Scrum* is quite simple, as well as its practices, artifacts, and rules. According to Massari (2016, p.241), "*Extreme Programming* (XP) is an agile software development methodology that, when used with *Scrum* software development management, can generate a very powerful result in software projects". Therefore, as a suggestion to improve the efficiency and effectiveness in the software development process it is advisable to combine the methodologies. Depending on the project approach, organizational culture, team size, product and project requirements etc., it is possible to apply the advantages of each of the methodologies.

2.2.3 Proper selection of agile software development methodologies

Let's look at other agile software development methods, *FDD*, *DSDM*, Crystal and comparisons with Scrum and XP methods.

The FDD (*Feature Driven Development*) method is a feature-focused, agile software development method focused on small iterations that usually last 2 weeks, where at the end a part of the system is delivered working. The *FDD* method is a method that consists of designing a prototype of the product, assembling a list of functionalities of that product and planning and developing by functionalities. It promotes the "phasing" of the project by functionalities (MASSARI, 2014).

Dynamic Systems Development Method (*DSDM*), according to Pressman (2016, p 79), comments that the method is an agile software development approach that provides a methodology for building and maintaining systems that meet tight time constraints through the use of incremental prototyping in a controlled design environment. For Massari (2014, p.22) the *DSDM* method considers the life cycle of a project with four phases: feasibility study, iteration of the functional model, design iteration and construction and implementation.

The Crystal method, according to Massari (2014, p.19) corresponds to:

> "a family of methodologies designed for projects led by small teams developing low-critical projects or even large teams developing high-critical projects. The main principles are: frequent delivery, reflective improvements (check for improvement paths and implement them), osmotic communication (close teams for sharing), personal security and focus".

A question that many developers, project team leaders and software engineers make: What is the methodology that we will use for this project? chart 7 - "comparison between the agile methods", presents the results of the criteria in Scrum, XP and other methods like FDD, Cristal Family and DSDM. The compared methods that meet the criteria of the agile manifest were XP, Scrum and Crystal, while *DSDM* and *FDD* partially meet.

Table 7 - Comparison of agile methods

Criteria	FDD	Scrum	XP	Crystal Family	DSDM
Self-organizable teams	No	Yes	Yes	Yes	Partly

Absence of phases in the development process	No	Yes	Yes	Yes	No
Minimum planning	No	Yes	Yes	Yes	No
Scalability	Yes	Yes	Yes	Yes	Yes
Refactoring	Not emphasized	Yes	Yes	Yes	Yes
Interactive and Incremental	Yes	Yes	Yes	Yes	Yes
Progress is measured by delivering the increments	No	Yes	Yes	Yes	Yes
Simple Project	A little bit	Yes	Yes	Yes	Partly
Effective engagement with the customer	Yes, but not emphasized	Yes	Yes	Yes	Yes
Adaptable customer relationship	Yes	Yes	Yes	Yes	Yes
Changing requirements	No	Yes	Yes	Depends on the type of project	Yes
Frequent inspections	Yes	Yes	Yes	Yes	Yes

Table 8, "Features Among Agile Methods", below, shows the key posts, main features and limitations among the XP, SCRUM, DSDM, FDD and Crystal methods.

Table 8 - Characteristics among agile methods

Methods	Key posts	Main features	Limitations
XP	Customer-driven development, small	Refactoring the system improves performance	Little attention to the use of

	teams and frequent versions.	and is responsible for the changes.	management practice.
SCRUM	Small, self-organizable, development cycle of up to 30 days.	Well defined and repeatable product view.	Lack of integration and acceptance tests in the development cycle
FDD	It consists of five processes and short iterations.	Simple method, development by characteristics and object modeling.	Focus only on design and implementation.
Crystal	Several methods with different characteristics.	Ability to select the most adaptable method for the project.	Difficulty in using estimates.
DSDM	Team with autonomy to make decisions.	It uses prototyping and has several roles for the execution of an activity in the method.	Only team members have access to the method's procedures.

As seen, it is important to have the knowledge of the main characteristics and limitations of the main agile software development methodologies, so that it is possible to select the most appropriate methodology for the project.

2.3.4 Agile methodologies based on industrial production

Software engineering and software development methodologies were inspired by manufacturing processes to consolidate their working methods. These manufacturing processes emerged from management theories and production methods (Fordism and Taylorism) born in the second half of the 20th century (PRIKLANDNICKI, WILLI and MILLANI, 2014).

The classical approach to administration was conceived in two independent streams, developed in different places, authors and principles, scientific administration and classical theory. Scientific administration, developed in the United States with the work of Taylor, where, according to Chiavenato (2004, p. 3) "was concerned with increasing the efficiency of the company through its organisation and the application of the general principles of administration on a scientific basis".

The classical theory was developed in France through the work of Fayol, where, according to Chiavenato (2004, p.4), the concern was to increase the efficiency of the company through the form and disposition of the organization's departments and their structural interrelationships, i.e., predominant attention to the organizational structure, to the elements of administration and departmentalization.

Fig.33 below shows the unfolding of the classical approach to administration into two theories: the scientific approach defined by Taylor with emphasis on tasks, and the classical theory defined by Fayol with emphasis on structures.

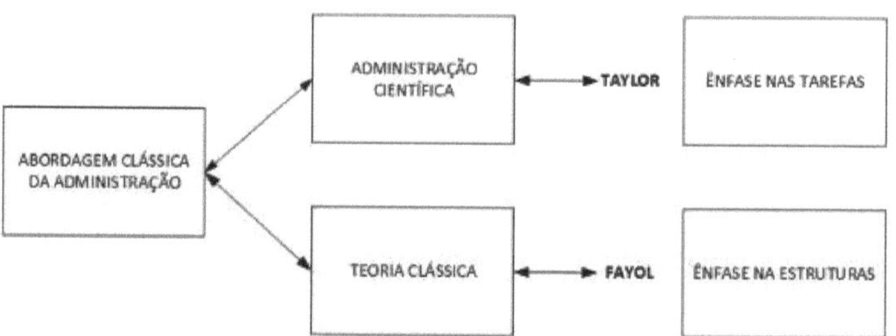

Fig. 33 - Breakdown of the classical approach
Source: Chiavenato (2006, p. 4)

In relation to Taylor's theory, focused on the emphasis of tasks (Fig. 33) Gilbreth (1868-1924) accompanied Taylor in his study by human effort, introducing the study of the times and movements of workers as a basic administrative technique for the rationalisation of work and concludes that all manual work can be reduced to elementary movements (*therbligs*).

These elementary movements make it possible to decompose and analyse any task, i.e. a task is divided into procedures or steps for its execution (work instruction). These steps are execution verbs, or Gilbreth's elementary movements (*therbligs*) as we have already seen in item 1.1, in table 3. With the aspect of division of labour, these procedures are also divided by the operation function (execution) and (administration) management.

The analysis and study of these procedures, in relation to time and their movements can increase the efficiency of the worker (correct use of available resources), whose functions are specifically the elements of the administrative process for the work of an administrator, manager or supervisor. In this sense, Fayol's theory defines general principles of administration, with emphasis on structures (Fig. 33), which complete Taylor's theory, and are:

1. Division of labour (specialisation of work increases work efficiency, i.e. it is the assignment of specific tasks to each individual, resulting in specialisation of functions and separation of powers).

    Authority and responsibility (authority consists of the right to order and the power to enforce. Responsibility is the duty to obey orders).

    Discipline (consists of respecting the rules and agreements established between the organisation and its agents).

4. Command Unit (each employee must have only one boss and one programme for a set of operations that aim at the same objective).

5. Management Unit (a head and a plan for a set of activities with the same objective).

6. centralisation (the administration must centralise decision-making).

7.   team spirit (management should promote team spirit, as it creates an environment and unity in the organization).

Over time the many ideas, approaches and techniques used in the essential processes, which directly produce the products in the industrial sector, could be applied in the production of services and in the essential processes related to production such as purchasing, physical distribution, after-sales services, etc. Currently the term operations and process management has been used in the organisational structure as a whole (SLACK et al., 2013). The operations functions consist of activities of the organisation for the production of goods and services such as cutting, transport, assembly, painting, etc.

Each company has an operations function, because each one produces some mix of products and services. The characteristics of the operations are described in table 9 below, regarding the cycle, identification, structure, results and its set.

Table 9 - Characteristics of operations

Characteristics of operations	
Cycle	Continuous, Repetitive
Identification	By function (Example: the cutting operation is related to the function of the cutting operator)
Objective	It maintains the business and describes the tasks of organisations.
Structure	Composed by activities and has input, processing and output (performs transformation). They use instructions to describe
Results	They generate products and services.
Set of operations	Process

Operations, strictly speaking, have always had to be managed, as there have always been organisations generating and delivering value packages to customers, whether this is happening explicitly or not. Currently, due to high competitiveness, organizations are seeking efficiency in production operations and using modern methodologies. One of these methodologies is related to the concept of *lean* production and management philosophy, called *Lean Manufacturing*. For Gronovicz et. al. (2013, p. 50), "the TPS system, also known as Lean *Production or Lean Manufacturing*, began effective in Japan in the 1950s, more specifically in Toyota".

For Cogan (2012, p.6) "the term *Lean* comes as a consequence of a production method that requires half the human effort, half the manufacturing space, half the investment and half the engineering hours to produce a new product in half the time". Table 10 below compares Henry Ford's mass production (Taylor and Fayol application) with lean production (*Lean*).

Table 10 - Characteristics of traditional and lean operations

Base	Henry Ford	Toyota
Project Staff	Specialised professionals	Teams of multi-specialised workers from all levels of the organisation
Production Staff	Non-specialised or semi-specialised workers	Teams of multi-specialised workers from all levels of the organisation
Equipment	Expensive, dedicated machines.	Manual and automatic systems that can produce large volumes with a wide variety of products
Production Methods	Making large volumes of standardised products	Making products that the customer is asking for
Organisational Philosophy	The responsibility lies with the	Value streaming using appropriate levels of empowerment - pushing

	hierarchical manager	responsibility down the organization
Philosophy	Objective is "good enough	The goal is "perfection

Today, companies work in fast-changing, global, interactive, innovative and employee-value environments, i.e. they operate through "agile thinking". In the case of software production, according to Cruz (2015, p. 12), the manifesto for agile software development, or simply the agile manifesto, was collaboratively created by the 17 professional representatives of development methods who were present at the 2001 meeting in Utah, western United States. As for software production, *Lean* methodology has brought significant advances through a lean software development process, let us look at details of *Lean agile* methodology and others that have migrated from industrial production processes.

2.3.5 *Lean* Software Method

Lean software production is based on lean principles such as (1) eliminating waste, (2) strengthening the team, (3) quick deliveries, (4) optimizing the whole, (5) building quality, (6) postponing decisions and (7) expanding knowledge. Table 11 presents these principles.

Box 11 - Lean principles of software development and management

Lean **Principles of Software Development and Management**	
(1) Eliminate waste	<ul><li>Partly done work: the famous "It's ready, just need testing". Define "the ready" well, avoiding rework.</li><li>Extra processes: "heavy" documentation that does not add value to the final software.</li><li>Extra Features: do not develop features not required by the customer/end user to please you.</li><li>Change of task or multitasking: Reduce the alternation of tasks, because the brain has a time to disconnect from one task to and concentrate on another. You should focus on the task.</li></ul>

		Waiting: the waiting time for the customer to approve the software is idle time. Until the software is homologated the development resources cannot be released until the project is finished. • Communication efforts: large or geographically distributed teams require good communication management. • Defects: fixing *bugs* takes time from the project.
(2) Strengthenin g the team	•	I work with the team in a self-organized and self-managed way.
(3) Quick Delivery	•	Maximize the Return on Project Investment by delivering the software quickly and continuously.
(4) Optimising the whole	•	Alignment with the objectives of the organization and delivery of the completed software.
(5) Building quality (ensuring quality with techniques)	•	Testing (unitary through test oriented development - TDD). • Refactoring: Improve and refine the code (lean code with the same behaviour). • Continuous integration: automatic compilation of the code repository, checking that the code entered has not hindered other software features.
(6) Postponing decisions	•	Leave decisions and commitments to the *Last Responsible Moment*, allowing information gathering and experience to strengthen decision making.
(7) Expanding knowledge	•	Prioritize continuous communication and *feedback* between teams and users during the software development process.

Source: Massari (2014, pp.24-25).

In the study of *Lean* practices as an "agile methodology" for software development and management, it is common practice that the migration from Lean *Manufaturing* to *Lean Software* (capture of Lean principles) is done through similarities and comparisons of production and development principles, respectively. It is therefore possible, through *Lean* development principles, to use similarities between production (Lean Manufaturing) and *Lean Software Development* (LSD), demonstrated in table 12, "similarities between lean production and effective product development.

Table 12 - similarities between lean production and efficient product development

Enxuta Production	Enxuto Development
Frequent Setup Changes	Frequent product changes (software releases)
Shortened manufacturing times	Shortened development times
Reduced stocks between stages of manufacture	Reduced information between stages of development
Frequent transfer of small batches of pieces between the manufacturing stages	Frequent transfer of preliminary information between stages of development
Reduced inventory requires resource clearance and a greater flow of information between the manufacturing steps	A short timeframe requires resource looseness and a greater flow of information between development steps
Adaptability to changes in volume, product *mix* and *design design*	Adaptability to changes in product design, schedules and cost targets
Broad task allocation for workers results in higher productivity	A broad assignment of tasks for engineers (developers) results in increased productivity.
Focus on rapid problem solving and continuous process improvement	Focus on frequent incremental innovation and continuous product and process improvement
Simultaneous improvement of quality, delivery times and productivity.	Simultaneous improvement of quality, development time and productivity.

Source: Proppendieck and Proppendieck (2011, p.38).

The *Lean Software Development (LSD)* methodology can be used in a complementary way with agile methodologies, *Scrum* approaches and XP, forming a hybrid development methodology.

While *Scrum* behaves as a *framework*, focused mainly on planning and management, XP enhances development practices in an interactive and intensive coding manner. *Lean Software Development*, on the other hand, comes with a set of principles, values and tools for lean development.

2.3.6 *Kanban* method

Another methodology migrated from production processes is *Kanban*. For Massari (2014, p.23), *Kanban* is a Japanese word meaning "sign" [visual card] and was adopted as a development methodology inspired by the Toyota factory system. It is basically a large whiteboard where tasks are written in post-its and go through various stages defined in the board, as shown in Fig. 34.

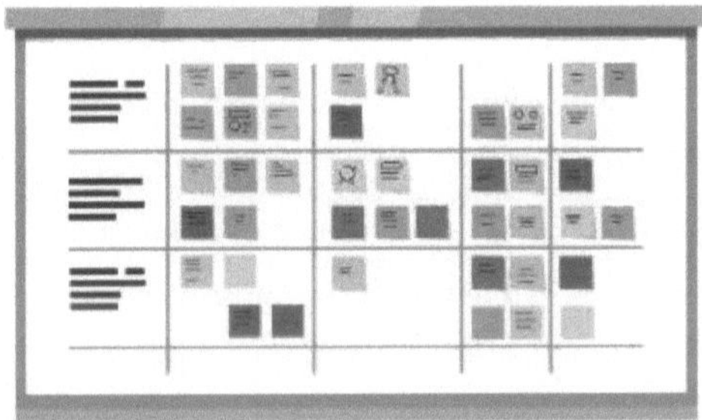

Fig. 34 - *Kanban* table
Source: freepik / iconicbestiary (2020)

Ortiz (2010, p.24) comments that Kanban used for half a century in manufacturing is a material replacement system that incorporates a symbolic language, instructions, to pull production, visual cues, scanners, cards, containers, etc., to help coordinate the transactions of materials and components throughout the factory and with suppliers. There are 6 principles of the *Kanban* base with respect to workflow, work quantity limitation, flow management, understanding of the process and cooperation in process improvement. According to Massari (2014, p.23) they are:

1. Workflow must be visible: it is important that the workflow is visible to everyone, so that it can be organised, optimised and tracked.

2. Limit the work in progress: it is important to limit this amount of work in progress because there are risks of creating "bottlenecks" in the process.

3. Managing the flow, to identify problems and improvements: the flow is not self-managed, so it is always important to be attentive to identify possible problems, changes and chances for improvement.

4. Ensuring clarity in the policies of the process: This makes the whole team aware of the rules of the game, avoiding any kind of misunderstanding.

5. Collaboration in process improvement: working as a team, always seeking to identify possible points for improvement.

According to the principles presented in the *Kanban* methodology, *it is* appropriate to have a *lean* and agile approach, as we have seen in the *Lean* approach (to dry tasks), and to combine the theory of constraints ("eliminating bottlenecks in the process"), both in the production of a physical product and of software. Fig. 35 illustrates the *Kanban* chart, which gives visibility to the development flow of a product or software, observing a sequential reference process.

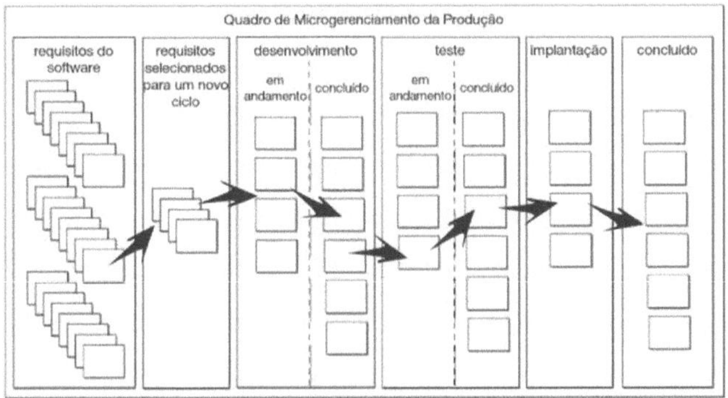

Fig. 35 - *Kanban* board that allows the visualization of the development flow through a reference process based on Kanban.

In short, *Kanban* is not a project management methodology, but a method that improves processes based on the visualization of the current and actual team process. It is through a board or panel, as illustrated in (Fig. 35), that the stages of software requirements, selection of requirements, development, testing, implementation and finalization are visually re-presented, in order to understand the entire software development process as well as its respective tasks.

According to Stellman and Greene (p.285) "everyone on the team should contribute to updating the Kanban panel to increase the probability of discovering extra stages that have gone unnoticed and thus create a more accurate view of the workflow".

2.3.7 *Scrumban* method

is the combination of the *Scrum* software management method with the *Kanban* task organisation and control approach. For Cruz (2015, p. 247), *Scrum* is a free practice and can be widely adopted to the needs of specific projects and organizations, but its panels, artifacts, events and rules should not be changed.

In *Scrum* software management, the *Kanban* panel also represents the control of the Time, which will basically have its exclusive flow, illustrated in Fig. 36. The *Kanban* panel is widely used in the Scrum software management method, specifically the follow-up of "*Sprint*" tasks and for the error corrections added by the customer and verified by the Time *Scrum*. For Cruz (2015, p.198) the flow sequence must be: first step, the customer identifies the errors and passes them on to the *Scrum team*; second step, these items go to the "*Backlog* of corrections"; third a member of the development team performs the correction and finishes the task and fourth step, the selected item follows the flow going directly to the "Done" column. See that in the *Sprint* task board of the control panel (Fig. 36), the *Sprint Backlog* are the users' stories and the tasks to be performed in the "to do" column, moving on to the next steps, in the "doing" and "done" columns.

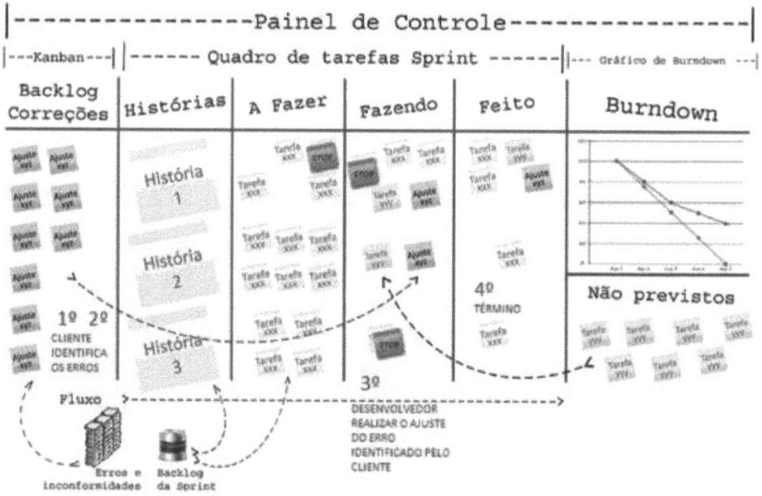

Fig. 36 - *Kanban* panel in *Scrum*
Source: adapted from Cruz (2015, p.199)

On the right side of the *Kanban* panel (Fig.36), a *Burndown* graph is shown. These are types of views that development and management teams use to monitor the progress of a *Sprint* and communicate a delivery of a software increment, called the *Sprint Burndown*.

For Priklandnicki and Orth (2009, p.154) the *Burndown* graph serves to track the progress and speed of the *Scrum* development team, whose progression panel also called the consumption graph, which illustrates the amount of features that have been developed so far in *Sprint*.

2.3.8 *Scrumban* + XP Method

For Pires (2016, p.21) the *Scrum* process is an agile method similar to XP, "as small teams, unstable requirements and short iterations to promote visibility for development. However the dimensions in Scrum differ from XP" (SOARES, 2016, p.5), but with a greater focus on management. As *Scrum* is a Framework, it works very well in combining or complementing different methods and practices established by the market. A strong adherence of this combination is that *Scrum* practices are used to manage several teams that use XP.

We can consolidate the characteristics of the *Scrum + Kanban +* XP (*Scrumban* XP) approaches as shown in table 13, which presents the main characteristics of each method and uses the best of their potential. For Gomes (2014) the idea is to use the programming engineering of teams in pairs and continuous integration of XP, in teams that use *Scrum.*

Table 13 - similarities between lean production and efficient product development

Consolidated features of Scrum + Kanban + XP approaches by team, individual and organization.	
Approach	**Team**
Scrum	<ul><li>Daily meetings.</li><li>Small teams.</li></ul>

	▪ Project prioritization.	
Kanban	▪ Team visualizes the task board and its flow. ▪ Time Scrum control. ▪ You can follow the *Backlog Sprint and Backlog* tasks of corrections.	
XP	▪ Programming in pairs ▪ Sustainable rhythm ▪ Collectivity. ▪ Code standardization, continuous integration.	
Organisational		
Scrum	▪ Each iteration package will generate the *Backlog sprint.*	
Kanban	▪ Determines the pace of a particular event ▪ No delivery iterations, the delivery is at the end. ▪ Prioritization and deliveries and any event has its own cadence. ▪ It has no iterations. ▪ Each stage of planning, prioritization, development and delivery has its own pace to better adjust to reality.	
XP	▪ Short deliveries ▪ User Tests ▪ Planning game ▪ United team	
Individual		
Scrum	▪ Fast staff. ▪ Team members answer basic questions, such as: What has been done? Is it difficult?	
Kanban	▪ Monitoring of tasks ▪ Individual visualization of the task of the whole process in terms of time dimension, execution and stage.	
XP	▪ Simple design. ▪ Test oriented development. ▪ Refactoring.	

Source: adapted from Gomes (2014)

In the combination of *Scrumban* + XP, the adoption of the *Kanban* approach aims to make the development process more transparent, stimulating a natural collection in search of problem solving and task execution. XP, on the other hand, emphasizes working in pairs (but can be adapted), constant communication, development by refactoring. With the adoption of *Scrum* as a task management tool, *a "Product Backlog"* is generated, and each release package of each software version will form the development team's *Backlog sprint* (list of tasks to be performed by *Scrum* team) (LINDERS, 2014).

Kanban can also be used with project management tools, such as *Jira*, which monitors activities and facilitates understanding of the development process. *Skam* (*Scrum + Kanban or Scrumban*) is focused on mobile device software development and uses the practical *Kanban* and *Scrum* basis. It is possible to visualize the workflow (development cycle of a customization "task") using the *Jira* tool and the *Kanban* panel.

However, it is possible to combine software development methods, with software process management approaches such as *Scrum*, and good project management practices. Let's see over the next topics how project management together with software development methods can improve the software process, in terms of quality, efficiency and effectiveness.

2.4 Software Development Project Management

The complexity of software development processes is noticeable, which unfolds in several phases, from software specification to inspection tests. However, we are now entering a more unstable field than the software development processes, the planning, execution and control of these processes.

Fig. 37 - project meeting

Source: freepik / pikisuperstar (2020)

Fig. 37 illustrates a project team meeting. Quality and its management is a combination of three basic premises: cost reduction, increased productivity and customer satisfaction. For quality to exist, through these basic premises, and to be contemplated in its fullness of production, both in the quality of the product to be delivered to the client (software functionalities), and in terms of deadlines (product completion time), and costs signed in contract, it is necessary to manage it. For Sommerville (2011, p.414) software project management is an essential part of software engineering. Projects need to be managed, as software engineering is always on tight schedule budgets. Now let's look at the concept of projects, and how it is possible to manage a software development process through good project management practices.

Project management is the administration of the activities of a project, which is managed from its conception to its closure (project life cycle, Fig.38), different from the software life cycle. Project management is the planning, monitoring, control and steering of the scope, deadlines, costs, quality, risks of the project, whose leadership skills are necessary to conduct them.

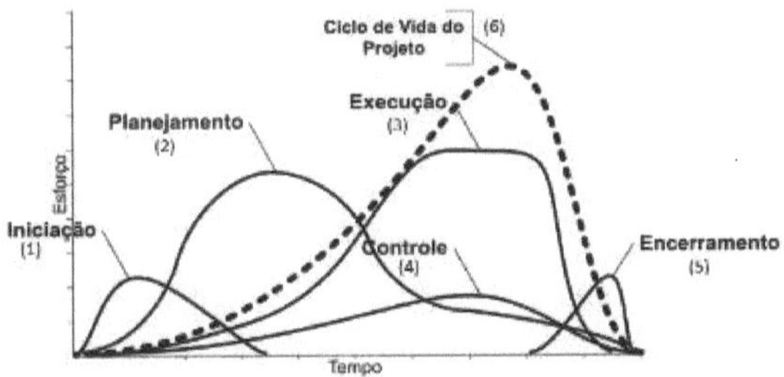

Fig. 38 - project life cycle

Source: Adapted from Vargas (2016, p. 34).

Fig. 38 shows the management of project planning from "initiation" (1), planning (2), execution (3), control (4) and closure (5), i.e. during the entire project life cycle, the scope, time and cost are planned, executed, controlled as well as can be changed due to changes occurring from possible risk factors. The greatest planning effort occurs at its peak (2) when the project plans are drawn up.

In modern project management, deliveries of tangible products and intangible products, called single products or deliverables to a customer, are made. Tangible deliveries are physical products such as civil construction, manufacturing of products and equipment, implementation of communication networks with respect to infrastructure and equipment. The project deliveries of intangible products are related to the concept of information, such as research and development, consulting, software, systems analysis projects and database (logical part of the project, such as modeling and diagramming).

Generally, projects involve the areas of engineering, supplies and works, where each area may have a greater or lesser performance in the context of the project. The engineering area is constituted by the functions of product specifications (software) or services, the area of supplies that consists of the purchasing functions for the production of the product, and the area of works, the activities of creation or development of the product or execution of the service. The functional areas act as service providers to the project, where the circles are the areas, the intersections are the areas of project management. If the supervision of each area is in accordance with the plan, it can be carried out in the same way. This can be an external or internal contract. The areas can interact where each area respects what has been specified for each. Finally, there can be an integration of project planning activities, schedule, costs, personnel management, risks, etc.

Another important aspect of project management is related to its life cycle. A project has its start time, planning, execution time and closing time, different from the life cycle of a software product or software process. These "times" are called the project life cycle and are composed of three main phases such as: inspiration, design or product design, development and delivery. These phases can also be defined as (1) beginning of the project; (2) organization and preparation; (3) execution of the planned work; and (4) completion. There may also be a pre-project phase, called pre-project. In this phase a feasibility study or an evaluation of ideas is carried out and turned into project proposals. Please note that there is no single approach and everything depends on culture, maturity, complexity, knowledge and degree of familiarity, infrastructure, integration, organisational structure, uncertainty, context and other factors. However, the main factors in the projects are related to the variables:

- Complexidade;
- Incerteza;
- Grau of familiarity;
- Contexto and difficulty.

The complexity in a project is linked to the number of variables it contains, such as human relations (relational complexity, linked to behaviour) and technical issues in a project (degree of difficulty in building a product). Another variable that undermines the complexity of a project is the complexity of its management, i.e. control of the scope, time, costs, risks, people and integration of the project, the responsibility of the project leader (Fig.39).

Fig. 39 - project management
Source: freepik / stories (2020)

The complexity of managing a project ranges from a simple project to the most complex, and the greater the interaction between areas the greater the complexity. With regard to the uncertainty in a project, this component is linked to the lack of knowledge about the objectives, scope, deadlines, project methods (lack of necessary information). The greater the lack of knowledge about these components, the greater the risks and uncertainties. The degree of familiarity or maturity is linked to familiarity with the projects, tools and requirements for project management.

Chart 14 below illustrates the main phases, divisions and artifacts of project management.

Chart 14 - Project life cycle, its divisions and artifacts used.

Project phase	Divisions	Artifacts used

Pre-project	Idea or *Brainstorming*; Design; Evaluation of ideas; Presentation.	*Briefing;* Feasibility study or prototype.
Project start	Presentation of the proposal; Acceptance/approval of the project.	Project Charter or Opening Term or Commercial/Technical Proposal EAP (Project Analytical Structure) or WBS (Work Breakdown Structure).
Organisation and preparation (Planning)	Product design or design.	Project Plan + EAP (Analytical Project Structure) or WBS (Work Breakdown Structure). Communication plan and/or stakeholder matrix; Risk Plan; Other plans; Contracts.
Implementation	Stages of development; Delivery.	Timeline, indicators.
Closure	Formal and contractual conclusion. List points of success and failure (lessons learned).	Term of closure.

In table 12, the discovery of the idea or inspiration (*brainstorming*), which is part of the beginning or the pre-project, is the moment where the idea arises from the need or opportunity arising from a strategic plan, a customer order or the existence of a problem identified in the company, sector or process of a product or service. Specifically for the study of this discipline, the project needs would be those of system improvement and definition of software and database projects for these systems, both as customizations and implementation.

The conception of the project, which is also part of the beginning of the project, turns this idea into a mental model using mental maps, briefing and other artifacts. This stage is part as a pre-project, where an evaluation or viability of these ideas is made. At the project start phase, the *Project Charter,* presented by the *PMBOK, is* made, which should contain information about the project scope and its main time constraints, budget, human resources, etc. (Fig. 39), The *Project Charter* is a project document (Fig.40), based on a prior and estimated sizing of scope (client requirements), time, cost, risks, assumptions, restrictions, steps, stakeholders and signatures.

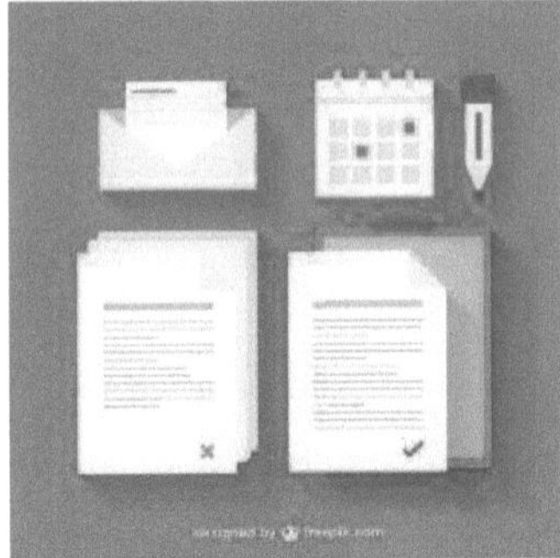

Fig. 40 - Proposal or Project Charter is a previous document
Source: freepik (2020)

Still at this stage, presentations of the product idea and the Project charter are made to the sponsor and others involved in the project, called *stakeholders.* It is important to note that a part of the software specification (requirements) of the software development process is carried out at the initial stage of the project (pre-project/start-up).

Once the idea(s) and the main project information have been accepted, the product design or design phase, organisation and preparation of this project begin. Detailed project plans are then drawn up, such as the project plan, analytical project structure (EAP) or WBS (work breakdown structure) (Fig. 41), communication plan or *stakeholder* matrix (those involved in the project), risk plan and other plans needed to detail the project structuring effort.

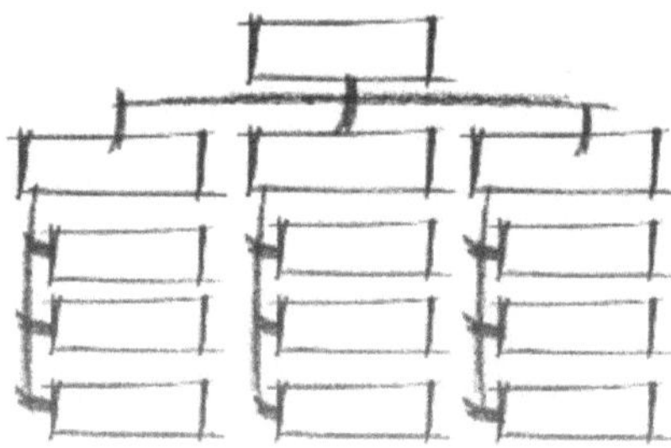

Fig. 41 - Analytical Structure of the Project (EAP)
Source: Pixabay / geralt (2020)

The artifacts required for the project, i.e. the amount of documents required for project definition, follow-up, control and closure, depend on several factors, such as the size of the project, the business involved, the time and need for planning, and the combinations with other best practices in project management and process management. The next phase in the project life cycle is project implementation. In this phase the gradual development of the product and its expected deliveries (defined in the EAP) to the client is carried out. It is at this moment that the software development process is applied, that is, the software specification stages (appears in two moments, beginning of the project and in the execution phase), design and implementation, software validation. Finally, there is the closing or closing phase of the project, where the project is formally and contractually closed, as well as the records of the lessons learned from success or failure.

2.4.1 Relevance of projects

For Veras (2016,p.1) the projects now play a key role in the evolution of the business environment, increasing productivity and improving management efficiency. Project management is now a recurring theme for all organizations and several methodologies are suggesting to improve the technique. "To meet demands effectively in an environment characterised by the incredible speed of change, a management model based on the focus of priorities and objectives becomes indispensable" (VARGAS, 2016, p.3).

In this sense it is necessary to use good practices and methods capable of developing the capacity for high project management in various market and business segments, especially in the area of public security and legal services, software development processes, optimization of social processes and others. To this end, the main practices in the market, such as PMI (Project Management Institute, PRINCE2 and ISO 21500:2012) guide and define methods, processes and good practices for successful projects. PRINCE2, for example, is a more widely accepted generic non-proprietary method of project management, offering a general *framework* for project work (OGC, 2011, p.4).

Before starting a project it is necessary to have some business need, to achieve strategic goals or any other organisational need. However, a feasibility study and evaluation of ideas that are transformed into project proposals and consequently actions is required. (RABICHINI JUNIOR and CARVALHO, 2013, p.31). Only after a technical and financial feasibility study has been carried out is the project initiated. Initiation only begins when the project is selected as viable. After the planning phase, the implementation process is triggered by the coordination of personnel and resources for the implementation and completion of the project. For Carvalho (2015, p.42) the objective of this phase is to satisfy customers and stakeholders in the project and is constituted, according to the PMBOK, the processes of integration, quality, human resources, communications, procurement and stakeholders.

2.4.2 Areas of Knowledge

According to Xavier (2016, p.31) The management processes (initiation, planning, execution, monitoring and control and closure) by PMI are organized and grouped into knowledge areas:

Integration of project management.

2.   project scope management.

3.   project time management.

4.   Managing project costs.

5.   project quality management.

6.   Human resource management of the project.

7.   project communications management.

8.   project risk management.

9.   project procurement management.

Many authors have carried out the didactic explanation of this project management, through these 9 (nine) management groupings.

The area of knowledge integration involves the integrations of activities necessary for the development and implementation and modifications of the plan. The scope management area (what will be produced and deliverable, deliverables, functional requirements of a software) deals with the monitoring and control of the limits of the requirements, deliveries and work packages through the analytical structure of the project (EAP), defined in the project plan. This scope management must follow a strategy plan as commented Camargo (2018, p.19):

> "The scope management plan should include the planning of strategies to manage the scope of the project with information on specific forms used to record information on scope, processes and procedures to collect, document and track project requirements as well as processes and procedures to build the project's CAS and its respective dictionary".

In Box 15, Camargo (2018) shows the scope activities and planning documents, and the scope management requires the activities of defining strategies, scope boundaries, project requirements and the definition of deliverables (the EAP structure and the details of deliveries):

Box 15 - Activities to plan the scope.

Activities to plan the scope	Documents generated
Planning strategies to manage the scope	Scope Management Plan
Define scope boundaries	Scope Statement
Define project requirements	Documentation of Requirements
Define main deliveries	Project Analytical Framework (EAP)
Define the work packages	EAP Dictionary

Source: Camargo (2018, p.19)

We have seen that to develop and deliver a deliverable product it is necessary to define the scope, i.e. "what to deliver?" and define a way to manage this delivery (the main deliveries and work packages). However it is also necessary to define "when to deliver?" is a way to manage the time of these deliveries. For Maximiano (2010, p. 86), the definition of activities is the basis for managing project deadlines - or time, this definition is developed in EAP -

project analytical structure and the main tool for managing deadlines is the schedule, i.e. deadlines and related activities.

In table 16, Camargo (2018, p.20), shows the activities to plan the time and documents generated. A management plan is defined for project time management. A schedule is defined for the definition of the activities, which includes the identification and sequencing of activities, the estimation of resources and the duration of project activities. The time management area aims to monitor the project deadlines by means of the time frame, defined through the project plan, from the elaboration, identification, sequencing of the activities and the estimation of the resources for the activities (CAMARGO, 2018).

Table 16 - Activity and documents in time planning.

Time planning activities	Documents generated
Drawing up the time management plan	Time Management Plan
Identify activities	Schedule
Sequencing activities	
Estimate resources for activities	
Estimate durations for activities	

Source: Camargo (2018, p.20).

The area of cost management processes is that which involves planning and controlling the estimated resources of project activities. In table 17, Camargo (2018, p.21) shows the activities to plan costs. For cost management a plan of cost collection and control procedures is defined. Cost estimation and budgeting activities are defined and cost estimate documents and budgets are prepared. The cost management area is related to the monitoring of project costs through the EAP artefact, including the costs of direct, indirect, fixed and variable activities as defined by the project plan (CAMARGO, 2018).

Table 17 - Activity and documents in cost planning.

Activities to plan costs	Documents generated
Define survey procedures and cost control	Cost Management Plan
Estimate project costs	Cost Estimates
Budgeting the project	Budget

Source: Camargo (2018, p.21).

The area of quality management involves ensuring that stakeholders' expectations are met. This management is carried out through quality assurance activities, standardization tools and quality monitoring and control during the project. The adoption of software development methodologies, software metrics, application of maturity levels and auditing are ways of improving and assuring software quality, within a project management approach (Fig. 42), through teamwork tasks, auditing tasks, consulting and meetings.

Fig. 42 - Quality activities and procedures
Source: Pixabay / geralt (2020)

The human resource management area of the project involves the responsibilities of providing sufficient resources to achieve project objectives. The communication management area aims to monitor communications between stakeholders through the communication plan, which contains the project-specific records, media and forms of communication (CAMARGO, 2018).

2.4.3 Reasons and benefits of project management

Organizations such as industry, commerce and service delivery are realizing their objectives through the project approach. Strategies are used to visualise where organisations want to go. The processes enable organisations to move towards achieving their goal, but it is the projects that make the planned actions of the strategies effective. The strategy is the basis for organisational decision-making, such as the decision to implement a new product or service, or to implement new administrative systems. Strategies are made effective by an action plan, which is carried out either through a project or portfolio, or by a programme (set of projects). However, it is important to note that one of the reasons for using a project approach and management is the strategic organisational alignment. This creates pressure to make the necessary efforts to achieve the proposed project objectives. In this way efficient projects and objectives aligned with the organisational strategy are desired. For Guedes, Fonseca and Maximiano (2011), implementation through competent management of the corporate project portfolio is one of the critical factors for long-term success and for building sustainable competitive advantages. In this sense, in the face of numerous projects, scarce resources or competition for resources, existing opportunities, set of delayed projects, lack of broad vision, and the pressures of those involved from the management and PMO (*Project Management Office*) project offices, questions should be raised such as: Which projects should be approved and prioritized? What criteria should be assessed for this decision making? How should resources be allocated to each project?

Before we manage projects, Maximiano (2010, p.34) comments that the first step is the correct choice of the project: In the process of choosing projects to be carried out, it is necessary to ensure that the projects chosen are effectively aligned with the strategy, that only the best ideas are transformed into projects and that, once implemented, the projects can be managed in a systemic way, becoming part of the portfolio or project portfolio, based on criteria and procedures of analysis and selection. In view of these issues, it is important to highlight the main objectives of portfolio management. For Junged, Barbalho e Silva (2014, p. 11), he highlights three objectives:

●Alinhamento of the projects with the company's strategy: it consists of translating the company's strategy into a set of projects that are really aligned with the achievement of the business objectives.

●Maximização of value: aims to optimise the relationship between resources used and expected returns with the project.

●Balanceamento/equilibrium between projects: this is a performance target which aims to establish the balance of projects.

We will see below that the projects are considered to be mechanisms that implement the organization's strategic actions, based on and aligned with the organization's strategies through tactical, strategic and budgetary plans. For this, it is necessary to know the portfolio management processes aligned to the corporate strategic planning.

2.4.4 Aligning projects with the strategy

The portfolio management processes can be grouped into process groups: organization strategy management, portfolio planning and portfolio balancing, and these constitute the portfolio management processes. Table 18 presents these groups of project portfolio management processes.

Chart 18 - Project portfolio management process group

Portfolio Management Process Group			
Process Group		Processes	Definition
Strategic Management		Mission, Vision	The vision expresses the purpose of the entity, provides a long-term direction. The explicit mission because the organisation exists and what its contribution to the environment is. (FREZATTI, 2009)
		Strategic Planning	Administrative technique which, through the analysis of an organisation's environment, creates awareness of its opportunities and threats and of its strengths and weaknesses for the fulfilment of its mission and, through this awareness, establishes a purpose of direction that the organisation must follow in order to seize opportunities and avoid risks. (FREZATTI, 2009)
		Strategic Objectives and Indicators	They make it possible to monitor the company's mission in the long term (Frezatti, 2009). It consists of projections, product performance analysis, results projections, definition of fields of action; sales projections, etc. (SIQUEIRA E BOAVENTURA, 2012).
A L I N	Portfolio Planning	Identification of components/proj ects	It is the first step in the project selection stage, it is the identification of project ideas and the need to help support the business (KERZNER, 2016).

H **A** **M** **E** **N** **T** **O** **E** **S** **T** **R** **A** **T** **É** **G** **I** **C** **O**		Categorisation of components/ projects	Projects divided into categories, one for survival and one for growth, discussed by (KERZNER, 2016, p. 585).
		Component assessment/ projects	Use of formal methods to evaluate the set of projects, defined by Junged; Barbalho and (SILVA, 2015).
		Selection of components/ projects / Prioritisation of components/ projects	Project selection stage, where the prioritization and strategic adequacy is carried out. For (KERZNER, 2016) this stage is one.
	Portfolio Balance	Identification of Portfolio Risks	A portfolio risk analysis needs a broad view in line with the organization's strategic objectives. Opportunities should be capitalized on, threats should be minimized, market changes should be responded to, and the focus on critical activities should be strengthened (FREITAS, 2016,p.35)
		Portfolio Risk Analysis	
Project Management		Project Program Management	Project management is the control and monitoring of the life cycle of projects. Projects are generated from the elaborate and aligned strategies of strategic planning and project portfolio planning. At this stage, the set of projects (programmes) or individual projects is managed, measuring performance in terms of time, cost and scope.
		Performance measurement of project programmes	
		Closing of project programmes	

The strategic alignment takes place in the portfolio planning process group and in the portfolio balancing, after the definition of the mission, vision, strategic planning and strategic objectives and indicators. It is through the analysis of the internal environment (strengths and weaknesses) and external environment opportunities and threats, also called SWOT matrix, that the objectives, measures, goals and initiatives (strategic actions) are generated in four perspectives of the organization: financial, customer, internal processes and learning and growth.

The portfolio planning defines which projects will be selected and prioritized according to the corporate budget, controlled by the budget control process, Fig. 43. For Frezatti (2009, p.35):

> "The projects correspond to the investments proposed, analysed and decided as a result of the organisation's strategies [strategy process in Fig. 42]. The absence of this element makes it impossible to assess the overall financial adequacy of the strategies decided by managers, both in terms of results (profit or loss) and the desired financing capacity and risk. The project portfolio must be analysed and decided in such a way as to optimise the appropriate timing of the investment and must be supported by evaluation methods consistent with a monitoring process".

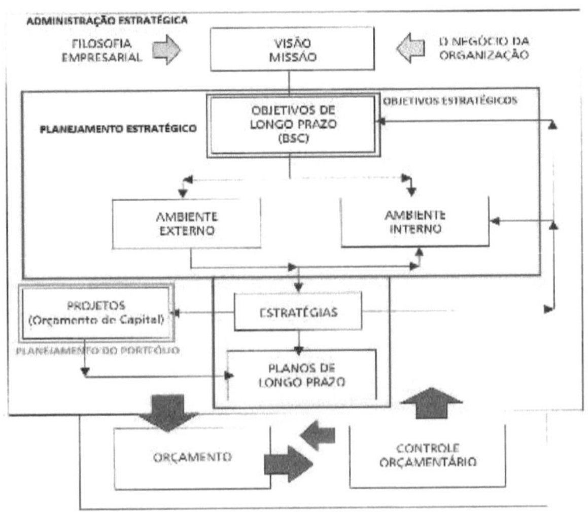

Fig. 43 - Strategy outline aligned with projects and budgets

Source: Pixabay / geralt (2020)

The "mission" and "vision" statements are the foundations of the strategies, but in order to form these statements we need analyses of an organisation's internal and external environments. The integrated understanding of the external and internal environments is fundamental to understand the present and the future and thus to develop strategies for decision making. The external environment undergoes continuous and rapid changes that can influence the strategies of organisations. The general environment is composed of influencing factors such as technological innovations, changes in laws, political scenarios, stock exchange, exchange market regulation, and others.

Within the process of designing and implementing a company's strategic planning, an analysis of the future state of the organization is required. Such an analysis uses strategic thinking, which in turn performs an environmental analysis and a forecast in the strategic planning process.

Fig. 44 shows a map of the steps in the process of setting up strategic planning using scenarios.

Fig. 44 - Process of setting up strategic planning using scenarios
Source: Adapted from Cavalcanti, Farah and Marcondes (2018).

Note in Fig. 44 that the first stage is related to identifying the current position of the organisation; the second stage is related to analysing the future state of the organisation; the third stage is linked to the development of alternative strategies; and finally, the fourth stage is related to decision making and implementation of the plan. Note that the configuration cycle is cyclical, i.e. it returns to the beginning of the cycle (stage I) for a new survey of information on the organisation's current position in relation to the current strategies. Step II determines the key factors for the organisation's success and the design of alternative scenarios. The next steps (III and IV) determine the development of the strategies through perspectives (financial, customer, internal processes and learning and growth) and the implementation of the plan for decision-making. Once the scenarios have been determined, the implications for each of them will be identified (CAVALCANTI; FARAH; MARCONDES, 2018, p. 49). The scenarios are determined using specific tools and help detect forces that change the future, as Cavalcanti, Farah and Marcondes comment (2018, p. 52):

> Scenarios are stories built on assumptions of what may happen in the future. Their construction must be planned, but not with the purpose of predicting the future, but with a search for different forces that can manipulate this future.

With this, we can say that scenarios are tools that support the organization in making decisions based on the visualization of a plausible future with greater or lesser probability of occurrence. Decision making can be supported by these tools and by methods of scenario configuration. Gonçalves (2011) states that scenario planning is different from forecasting: for the author, it points out possible futures without predictive goals, that is, it builds scenarios and identifies trends that materialize in the search for "possible futures" of the company's insertion environment configuration. Within the concept of scenarios, the time of analysis in a short period of time, also called the short time horizon of analysis, is that in which no drastic changes occur. In a long term horizon, drastic changes in the macroeconomic environment will occur more easily and disruptions are the most likely events to occur.

After the stage of identifying the organisation's current scenario, i.e. identifying how the strategies outlined are contributing to the achievement of the organisation's goals and objectives, it is necessary to carry out an analysis of possible future scenarios or forces that may act on the organisation and misalign its goals.

The graph in Fig.45 illustrates a projection of events over time through areas P (forecast), C (scenarios) and E (speculations). It can be seen that curve 1 represents the uncertain events; and curve 2, the predetermined events. Area P is a short-term area, in which a small number of uncertain events and a large number of predetermined events occur. In this area, then, predictive applications are possible. In area C, with a longer time, uncertain events increase and predetermined events decrease. This period is useful for applying the scenario methods, i.e. a greater study of trends. But note also that a very distant horizon, like area E, is full of speculations and high uncertainties and very few predetermined events. See below Fig. 45:

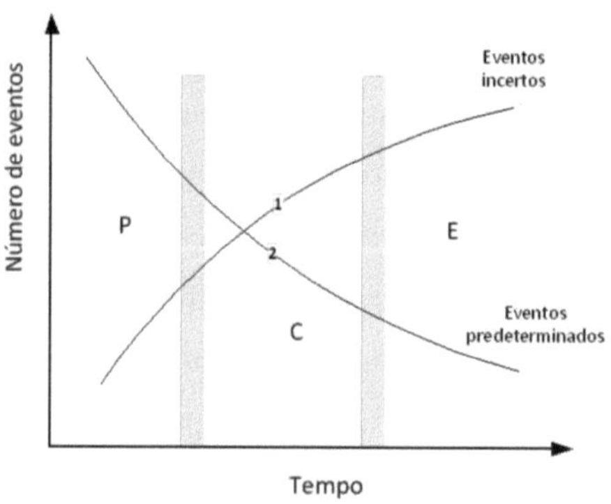

Fig. 45 - Projection of events over time
Source: Adapted from Heijden (2009, apud GONÇALVES, 2011)

Another stage of competitive intelligence, related to environmental analysis, is the analysis of competition, which corresponds to diagnosing and making comparisons with the competition to be faced. The *SWOT* tool (strengths, weaknesses, opportunities and threats) can be used to perform competitive analysis. The term is an acronym of the English language: S (*Strenghts*) = Forces; W (*Wekness*) = *Weaknesses*; O (Opportunities) = Opportunities and T (*Threats*) = *Threats*. SWOT is a tool used to perform environmental analysis and allow the exploration of alternative scenarios of the business environment for some years.

The forces are related to the advantages the company has over its competitors. Questions such as: What are your best activities in relation to your competitors? What are your best resources in relation to your competitors? What is your greatest competitive advantage over your competitors?

Let us look at the strengths, weaknesses, opportunities and threats:

- Weaknesses (weak points): weaknesses are the skills that interfere with or hinder the progress of the business in any way. Weaknesses or limitations identified in the internal environment that may restrict the organisation's performance are also considered.
- Strengths: these are facts, resources or other factors identified with the internal environment that can mean a competitive advantage or a differential in the fulfillment of its mission and vision.
- Opportunities: an opportunity is a condition in the general environment that helps the company to obtain strategic competitiveness or to prosper.
- Threats: threats are situations, barriers and obstacles arising from the external environment, existing or potential forces (which may occur) that are beyond the company's control and may impair its positioning and performance in the competitive environment.

Note that in Table 19, the crossing of the external factor "Opportunity" as an example of market growth due to increased income of the target audience, combined with the internal factor "Strength Point" as an example of the institutionally strong image of the organization, allows the company to launch new products at the same time as the current product is encouraged. The possible strategies that should be generated from this analysis of the internal and external environment should be focused on offensive development, making the best use of this crossover. Examples of strategies resulting from this crossover are the creation of new physical products and software, and the development focused on the growth of the sales volume of the current product. These strategies are called "development strategies".

In the crossover between the "Opportunities" relationship of information on market growth is related to increasing the income of the target audience, with the "Weaknesses" factor, whose raw materials are dependent on few suppliers, it is necessary to develop defensive strategies through growth actions. These actions would focus on more detailed investigation of competitors, sales growth, market share, business diversification, mergers and partnerships, vertical and horizontal integration. These strategies are called "Growth Strategies".

In the crossover between the "Opportunities" relationship of information on market growth is related to increasing the income of the target audience, with the "Weaknesses" factor, whose raw materials are dependent on few suppliers, it is necessary to develop defensive strategies through growth actions. These actions would focus on more detailed investigation of competitors, sales growth, market share, business diversification, mergers and partnerships, vertical and horizontal integration. These strategies are called "Growth Strategies".

Table 19 - SWOT Matrix and the types of strategies generated in the correlation of external and internal factors of an organization

	Demographic	Economic	Cultural Partner	Global	Technology	Political/Legal
	Factors external to the organisation					
	Opportunities (Opportunity) Market growth due to increased income of the target public			Threats (Threat) Entry of new external competitors through market opening		
Strong point (Strenghts) Ex: Solid institutional image	**Development** (Offensive - make the best use of them) 1. New products 2. Growth of current product sales volume. 3. New markets. 4. It no longer meets a single segmentation.			**Maintenance** (Adjust - restore strengths) 1. Carry out an advertising campaign based on the institutional image supporting the new products. 2. Dedication to a single product.		
Weak Point (Wekness) Raw material supply is concentrated in a few organisations	**Growth** (Defensive - closely examining competitors) 1. Market participation. 2. Growth in sales. 3. Diversification in business. 4. Mergers and partnerships. 5. Innovations. 6. Vertical and horizontal integration.			**Survival** (turn around) 1. Development of New Suppliers. 2. In a crisis scenario waste must be eliminated. 3. Liquidation of the business as: Expenditure reduction. Elimination of product lines. Personnel Reduction. Reduction in stock level. Equipment allocation. 4. Divestment of the business such as: Sales of Assets and sale of some units discarding units of negative results and remaining units of positive results.		

Internal factors in the organisation

After applying the SWOT tool for diagnosis and comparison with the competition, *Target* (targeted marketing) and *Marketing Size* procedures are carried out. The *Marketing Size* is the sum of the revenues generated by all members of a given economic segment. *Target Marketing* is the process by which advertisers carry out marketing strategies to meet the diverse needs of consumers, also called "target market choice". This choice consists of identifying markets with unmet needs, determining market segmentation, choosing a target market and positioning through marketing strategies. We have *Target Marketing*:

- Identification of unmet need markets: a group of consumers with lifestyles, behaviours, needs that improve knowledge about specific needs.

- Market Segmentation: is the division of a market into distinct groups with common needs that may correspond, in a similar way, to a given marketing action. Segmentation can be geographic, demographic, psychological, behavioral or benefit-based.

- Choosing a target market: the choice of segmentation analysis will show the available market opportunities such as determining the number of segments to enter. It will also show the determination of the segments offering the greatest potential.

Finally, after the market analysis, the characterization and validation of the Client is performed. In this activity important characteristics are considered such as differences in personality and consumer behavior, demographic dimensions such as age, gender, family structure, social class and income, and others. In the validation with the client a MVP (minimum viable product) is performed. The MVP is a set of initial tests made with the objective of performing a validation of the viability of a business or product. Through the

MVP it is possible to carry out numerous practical experiments that will be developed for the client, which can be partial or incremental.

After the validation stage, the business feasibility analysis is carried out, through an economic and financial feasibility study. In this last stage, the costs and revenues expected from the project are measured through financial statements (return on investment, NPV - net present value). This determines whether the business is feasible or not. The objective of the net present value of an asset (NPV) is to bring the value of the investments, for example, in an investment project, assuming that the FC (cash flow) is known. The NPV is the same as *net present value (*NPV) and is equivalent to discounted net cash flow. It is also the valuation method used to estimate the attractiveness of an investment opportunity. This financial analysis uses future free cash projections and discounts them to arrive at a present time value, which is used to evaluate the potential of an investment. Presenting a positive net present value means that the investment is viable because it offers a higher return than the discount rate.

Another strategic tool for analyzing the external environment can be used when organisations are behaving in relation to the development and implementation of strategies. An important question that should be asked to this behaviour is: how do *stakeholders* visualise the strategies happening? For Zaccarelli (2012, p.7) comments: "Those who know nothing about strategy see nothing of the company's current strategy. Those who know everything about strategy, see all the current strategy happening". Knowing about strategy is so vital for the survival of organisations that Zaccarelli (2012, p.8) presents some consequences of the need to "know" to see:

1. There is no point in asking an executive who is not familiar with the concept of strategy what the company's current strategy is.

   In a company, it is only worth discussing the current strategy as a group, to improve it, if all the participants in the group have the same knowledge about the strategy.

   If a strategy specialist submits a plan proposal for a new company strategy, executives who know little about strategy will not be able to appreciate and judge the proposal because they are not able to say whether the new plan will improve or worsen the existing strategy - which they don't even know exactly!

However, for the executive to visualise the strategies to happen, they need to be developed and implemented in a planned and efficient manner. For this strategic process to take place, the executive must identify what skills his company needs to gain competitive advantage in a constantly changing market. For this purpose Porter (1979) has developed a model for analyzing the competitive environment, providing the mapping of five competitive forces that allows the company to position itself more clearly. The five forces are customers, suppliers, direct competitors, new entrants, and substitute products, as shown in Fig.44. The battle for profitability in the production chain is horizontal, through the bargaining of customers and suppliers. The vertical relationship between established competitors and the threat of new entrants and the threat of substitute products/services (Carvalho and Laurindo, 2010) is observed.

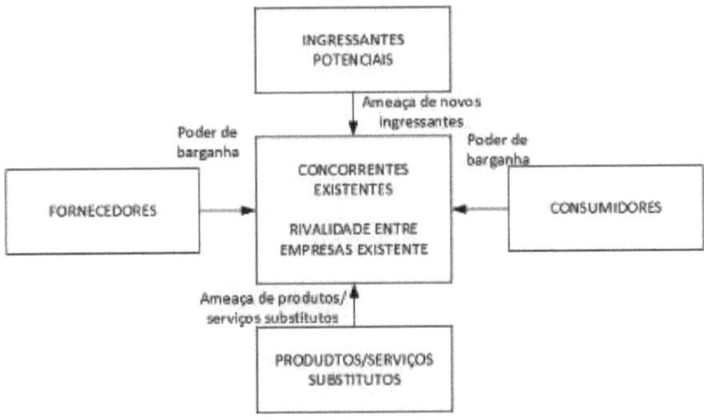

Fig. 46 - Porter's competitive forces

Source: Adapted from Carvalho and Laurindo (2010, p.43)

Through an analysis of Porter's competitive force structure (Fig. 46), it is possible to identify which of the competitive forces have the greatest impact on an industrial sector. When the structure is analysed, it is possible to verify that one of the forces in the industrial competitive environment stands out, and it is on this force that the strategy must be focused. With this, it is possible to carry out a strategic positioning that makes it possible to neutralise the force that stands out through strategies, thus obtaining competitive advantages. That is, after the structural analysis of the competitive forces, together with the analysis of the macro-environment (opportunities and threats) a structural analysis within the industry (strengths and weaknesses, skills, resources, technology) is carried out, in this case it is suggested to use the SWOT analysis matrix, and from its skills the appropriate strategies are generated. This process is called environmental analysis.

Another task that must be carried out in this process of strategy development is to align the goals. The strategies must be aligned with the mission, vision, objectives of the organisation, its goals to be achieved and the functions of a company.

For Pize (2015) With regard to the achievement of the strategic goals, while defined through the organization's internal and external diagnoses, the future scenarios developed according to a future vision, they must be feasible to be achieved and not merely wishes. They must be achievable, realistic, considering the resources and time available. Strategic objectives should be monitorable and controllable over time to verify that they have been achieved. For   each strategic objective, the organisation must   create measurement indicators that demonstrate whether it has been achieved. Targets should also be set for each indicator and the results of the indicators should be measured regularly. The results of the indicators should then be compared with the targets and corrective and/or preventive actions should be taken. Some examples of strategic objectives would be:

    -increase market share by 2%;

-Diminish   staff turnover;

-Raise   the number of new sales to customers.

A target for the market share indicator would be 2%, while that for the turnover indicator would be considered an ideal target of 100%, i.e. no turnover. For the new sales increase indicator it would be a considerable 30% or more. It all depends on the strategy implemented to be achieved for the future scenarios.

As far as functions are concerned, Barney and Hesterly (2011) comment that even the best formulated strategy is competitively irrelevant if it is not implemented and effectively when all functions of a company are consistently aligned with them. One example is a company where a particular sector, such as marketing, is not aligned with the cost leadership strategy. It may advertise products that it does not sell, i.e. it will sell products that are reliable (but not stylish) and cheap (but perform poorly), thus disappointing its customers. Therefore there must be alignment in all functional areas of a company. '

After the environmental analyses, configuration of the strategic planning using scenarios, positive signs of economic and financial viability and alignment of strategies, it is necessary to create a business budget and manage it according to project demands.

The projects are generated from the operational plans of the various sectors of the organisation and move on to the prioritisation and selection stage (project portfolio planning). These operational plans consist of budget forecasts and financial statistics and generate action plans for project execution within the software development process. Each action or set of actions in the plan may give rise to a project or a project portfolio.

The projects may involve various services and products that use various functional tasks of the organization, such as production projects, maintenance, new technology, assembly, diagnosis, implementation of systems, organizational change, consulting, system development, feasibility studies, research and development, investments in construction, renovation of physical structures, etc.

Project, portfolio and programme management are motivated by organisational strategies and pushed by the organisation to achieve project objectives. We will now look at the integration and scope processes as well as the tools for structuring the project scope.

2.4.4 Managing the scope of a project

We saw that the projects are generated from the organizational needs, from the analysis of the internal and external environment, the objectives and organizational strategies, generating a MVP and consequently a scope for the projects. Even so, it is a scope that must be polished, through early stages of the production process, in the case of software, such as the analysis of customer requirements (internal and external). A detailed planning of how the production management will be carried out. The planning stage of the project management takes place at a later stage in the project, after the conception of ideas and needs (conception and initiation). Fig. 47 shows the implementation phase of project management planning in the project life cycle, in which the "project management plan" is generated.

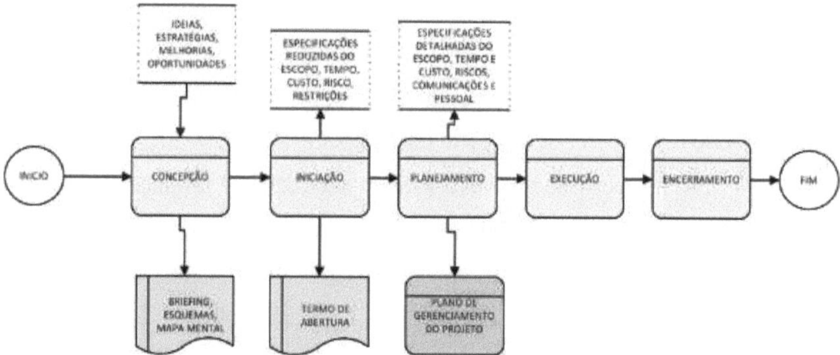

Fig. 47 - Planning stage of the project management after the conception and initiation of the project.

This project life cycle can occur in a more detailed way, as shown in Fig. 47 (traditional approach of PMI), or in a leaner way, through an agile management approach.

The project management plan contains the detailed specifications of scope, time, cost, risks, communications and project personnel, also called the "Project Plan" or "Specification Plan" (review item 2.1.1, Fig. 9, where it shows the activities of the requirements engineering process) and specification meetings with the client, (Fig. 48), must be aligned with the project planning to compose the time and cost of the activities, and is composed in

Scope Management Plan (detailed in sequence);

2.	time management plan;

3.	Cost management plan;

4.	Risk Plan;

Communications Plan;

6.	quality management plan;

7.	Human Resources Management Plan;

8.	procurement plan;

9.	Stakeholder management plan.

Fig. 48 - Meeting for project specifications
Source: freepik / stories (2020)

From this point on, a detailed planning of how the project will be implemented will be carried out in relation to the expectations and objectives sought in the project design. At the stage of drawing up the Project Plan, Mei (2014, p.83) comments that this is the opportunity for the parties involved to assess whether the needs and wishes have been taken into account in the conception, start of the project described in the opening statement, the risks that may occur in its implementation and whether the deadlines and costs are in line with expectations.

For Camargo (2018) The project management plan is an artifact where the project manager will integrate the different knowledge areas of the project. The integration consists of the coordination of the project so that the knowledge areas form a cohesive whole. The deadlines, for example, need to be integrated with scope and costs; the risks, on the other hand, need to be integrated with virtually all project areas. Integration is initiated in terms of openness, in which the needs of the project are initially assessed and planned in the project management plan.

For Maximiano (2010, p. 45), "scope management comprises the planning, execution and control of project products or deliverables. The project scope can also be understood as the scope of the project products". The project scope, i.e. "what does the customer want? what should be done? what product should be delivered? How should it be done?", initially occurs during the birth of ideas in functional sectors, through meetings, conversations, needs, internal and external opportunities and above all through the formalisation of the organisational strategies generated from strategic business planning.

Fig. 49 - Planning the project agenda
Source: freepik (2020)

The first step in scope administration (management) is scope planning. "The project planning starts with the design of the scope of work (Fig.49). This stage is responsible for creating alternatives (ways) of conducting the project. Its aim is to describe how the work will be carried out during the project so as to facilitate the construction of the project scope" (VARGAS, 2016, p.173).

This stage takes place at an early stage in the project start up (start of the project life cycle) and at another stage in the scope detailing. In the initial stage, the scope is elaborated with initial information at the opening of the project, which are formalized in an opening term or Project Charter, according to the PMI. This document is composed of important terms such as: needs, objectives, project scope statement, detailed scope and delivery structure through EAP/WBS (project analytic structure), project stakeholders, justification, constraints, assumptions as well as project time and costs. Fig. 50 presents the processes of the scope knowledge area according to the 5th edition of PMBOK, the planning of the scope management, the collection of requirements, the definition of the scope and the creation of the project analytic structure (EAP). Note that the flows are bidirectional for process improvement. For example, an adjustment made in adding requirements should be readjusted in all processes.

Fig. 50 - processes in the area of knowledge of scope
Source: adapted from the 5th Edition of the PMBOK.

In practice, the scope of a project starts from the initial ideas of the project, in its conception or preview, even in departmental meetings or corridor suggestions, however, it is from the elaboration of an initial formal document that the initial scope of the project is presented. The initial scope process consists of the authorisation of the initial project tasks. The business needs and the main requirements of the product or service must be documented in a formal document that authorises the start of the project, granting the project manager permission to use the resources.

This formal document can be called in different ways, such as "Project Charter" (a term that appears in the PMI references), "project opening term" or "project proposal" or "draft specifications". Its purpose is to initially structure the ideals in a macro formalisation of scope, time and cost, as well as the project objective, possible risks, assumptions, involvement and project steps. Depending on the approach and complexity of the project, more or less detailed planning is required. If the planning requires more detail, it is necessary to draw up a so-called "Project Plan". However, not every project needs this detailing, because for simpler projects of low complexity and easy to predict, monitor and control, only a few artifacts are required, or even only a Project Charter. In the sequence below, adapted from Vargas (2016, p.181), "the scope specification [in this case the opening term] contains the main specifications of scope, time and cost estimated in a macro manner, as well as those involved, objectives, justifications and possible risks".

Project title.

2. Name of the person who prepared the document.

3. Name of sponsor (support to project manager).

4. Name of the project manager and his responsibilities and authorities.

5. Preliminary organization chart.

6. Name of the members of the project team.

7. Project description.

8. Objective of the project.

9. Justification for the project.

10. Product of the project.

11. Customer/sponsor expectation.

12. Project success factors.

13. Premises

14. Restrictions.

15. Project boundaries and specific exclusions (all that will be addressed by the project);

16. Analytical structure of the project (upper levels of the structure);

17. Main activities of the project.

18. Main project deliveries.

19. Basic project budget;

20. Delivery plan and project milestones.

21. Initial project risks.

22. Configuration management requirements and project changes.

23. Registration of change in document.

24. Approvals.

For Camargo (2018,p.25), a project start can be further divided into two stages, pre-project (or project proposal) and the opening term: the type of documentation prepared in the pre-project proposals can vary, and depend on the company or organisation, and the type of product or service it works with.

Managing the scope is not the same as managing the project as a whole, but a part of it. The project is composed, according to its life cycle, of initiation, planning, execution and closure. The word manage means plan, execute, monitor and control. Therefore, the project manager will manage in these phases, the planning of scope, time and cost. He will also manage execution by monitoring and controlling this scope, time and cost.

For Camargo (2014, p.49) the scope management plan or scope plan should add action planning to manage the project scope with information on specific forms that will be used to record information on scope, processes and procedures specific to the collection, documentation and tracking of project requirements.

The stages of scope management range from project design to detailed scope. In this stage the artifacts are generated by the PM Mind Map elaboration processes, scope statement, requirements and detailing and EAP (analytical structure of the project). The development of the scope in the project and its artifacts have a dosage in terms of artifacts and detailed scope, depending on the complexity and approach of the project. In less complex approaches, only

PM Mind Map is enough for a better understanding of the project. There is a wide use in the project management area, regarding its scope, specifically used for complex projects, thus meeting the processes defined by PMBOK and PM Mind Map model. For projects of low complexity (regarding scope) it is possible to use even the PM Mind Map process. Besides the opening term, suggested by PMI, good practices of scope plan development, more detailed, are needed.

Camargo (2014, p.49) specific documentation targeted by the IMP, such as (1) scope statement to define scope boundaries; (2) requirements documentation to define project requirements; (3) project analytical framework (EAP) to define main deliveries and (4) and EAP dictionary development (last level EPA detailing) to define work packages. Both forms are attractive depending on the complexity, criticality, scope of the projects, where such artifacts can be used together or adaptable to the project.

For Maximiano (2010, p. 50), "the scope statement is a summary statement of the range of products or services to be provided to the customer. It is the first step in the process of establishing project deliverables". It is the explanation of what the project will do, or even what it will not do (requirements will not be met). It is a statement with steps and deadlines to be met. According to Vargas (2016), the scope statement is a detail of the preliminary scope statement, i.e. the project opening term. The PMBOK states that the degree and level of detail with which a project scope statement defines the work that will be undertaken and the work that will be excluded determines how effectively the management team can control the scope of the VARGAS project (2016, p.62).

Table 20, shows the artifact "scope statement" with the project scope specifications.

Table 20 - Scope Statement

TITLE OF DOCUMENT	
Project Name	
Date:	Document Version No.
I. Project title and description Definition of what the project will be called and what it will consist of.	
II. Sponsor Configuration of who will provide the financial resources for the realization of the project.	
III. Project Manager and Authority Confirmation of the role of the project manager and the type of organisational structure in which he will operate.	
IV. Team Definition of who will work on the project	
V. Objectives Confirmation of what the project is about, why it is being carried out	
VI. Justification Explanation of what is behind the project, what motivates the company to do it.	
VII. Success Factors List of Factors that will ensure the success of the project, i.e. what the project will need to be successful.	
VIII. Restrictions Definition of the factors that will limit the project's actions.	
IX. Premises Assumptions or assumptions that the manager states with regard to the project.	
X. Specific exclusions Description of what will not be done in the project	
XI. Main deliveries (scope included) Outline of what will be done with the project.	
XII. Budget envisaged Value allocated to the project.	
XIII. Main milestones Forecast of the project stages, with their expected completion dates. These dates are only reference dates and are subject to change after the official project schedule has been completed. They normally serve as references for the maximum dates at which that milestone [...] should be included.	

XIV. Project acceptance criteria. What the project will have to do to be accepted by the sponsor and other interested parties.		
Approved by:		
Signature:		
Record of changes: Date:	Requested by:	Description:

Source: Adapted from Camargo (2014,p.49).

The scope statement is a detailed *Project Charter* and must contain a description of the project, those involved in the project including project and support staff, project objectives, justifications, success factors, restrictions, assumptions, exclusions, key deliverables, planned budget, key project milestones, project acceptance criteria and approvals. The scope statement is a kind of initial contract that must have new additives added after further analysis of the scope, or may generate a more detailed contract depending on the needs and complexity of the project (Fig. 51). There may also be changes to the scope statement, and as many versions as necessary.

Fig. 51 - Scope statement or *Project Charter* is an initial contract

Source: freepik / iconicbestiaty (2020)

Camargo (2014) defines that before the detailing of the scope, the division of manageable parts, a documentation of requirements is necessary, the same as Mei (2015) presents in its *PM Mind Map* model, in the product perspectives. Camargo (2014, p.58) comments that "requirements are conditions that must be met by a system, product or component, a standard, specification, or other formal documents. The "requirements of a project" include the needs, wishes and expectations of the sponsor, customer and other parties". Within a software process, a customer's requirements will become functional (define the behaviour of the system) and non-functional (reliability, portability, usability, etc.). The project requirements are linked to the product requirements, even if they are different, because the time and cost of planning, execution, monitoring and control of a certain product or service resulting from the project is directly proportional to the functional requirements of this product or service. An example would be, the more functionalities or business rules a system, process or innovative product has, the more time and cost it takes to develop them

The requirements are the wishes of the customers regarding the project that will generate a product or service. The time, cost, resources themselves are project-specific requirements. At this stage it is possible to draw up requirements documents and a mental map to understand the needs of the product that the project will generate. The documents can be tables that control the requirements throughout the life cycle of the project.

One of the main reasons for changes after a project starts is the inclusion, modification, or exclusion of requirements. In this way, the manager's ability to collect all the requirements of the project before it is carried out reduces the probability of changes [...]" CAMARGO (2018, p.58).

Fig. 52 - Workshop is a form of collecting requirements
Source: freepik / rawpixel.com (2020)

For the process of collecting requirements, the project team can use various technical tools, such as: interviews, workshops [(Fig. 52)], group dynamics, surveys, etc., or collect requirements from documents such as: studies, orders or documented customer requests (BORGES and ROLLIM, 2015, p.43). A requirements documentation would be the combination of some requirements traceability matrix with mental maps or diagrams, which detail the requirements and the product of the project, making it clearer what is to be produced or developed for the customer, in accordance with the project team. For Camargo (2014, p.59), a very useful tool to collect and organize the requirements is the mind map. Mind Map is a *brainstorming* tool, also called Mind Map, assembling diagrams based on a central idea or image to survey solutions or possibilities for problem solving (Fig. 53).

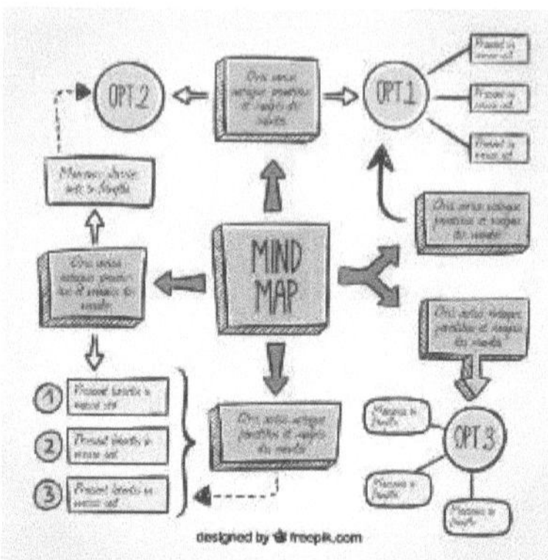

Fig. 53 - Mental Map

Source: freepik (2020)

There are several ways to present the scope of the project in this second stage of scope management. Ideally, a combination of best practices and PMI documents, and the use of tools that provide a better integrated visualisation of the project scope, should be undertaken. Or even depending on the use of agile software development methodologies (adaptive methodologies), if you use only little documentation (in a prescriptive way) and more visualisation, to quickly assimilate the requirements.

This visualization efficiency facilitates the control of its execution, being able to be reformed and adapted in time, without greater losses or addition of resources to the project. One of the visual tools that can be adapted to PMBOK, or used individually, is *PM Mind Map*. According to Mei (2015, p.83), PM *Mind Map* (Chart 21) is ideal for this purpose, with the use of all its perspectives and elements or only the perspectives conditions, execution and control, not allowing inconsistencies in the plan, caused by the long sequence and quantity of documents. With this combination it is up to the project leader or the specialists to define which and how many artifacts (documents) and perspectives will be necessary for the realization of the planning, be it scope, time, cost, restrictions, premises, risks, resources and deliveries.

Table 21 - PM Mind Map - Conditions Perspectives, Product.

Project:			Responsible (GP)
Business Outlook			
Value Proposition - Objective - Business Results			
Product Outlook			
Requirements - Product, service or result - Requirements			
Perspectives Influences			
Stakeholders and other internal influences			
Prospects Conditions			
Restrictions	Premises		
	Risks		
Outlook Implementation			
Resources	Delivery	Deliveries (period 1, period 2, ...period n)	Total Cost
Formulas	References and measurements	Result for period 1, period 2, period n)	Time and cost estimate

Source: Adapted from Mei (2015)

In Table 21, the specifications contained in *PM Mind Map* (*Project Model Canvas* type) are relatively the same as those of the PMI *Project Charter*, linked to business perspectives, perspectives of influences (interested and involved in the project) and execution perspectives (deliveries, results, resources, cost, formulas, references and measurements).

Another widely used tool for structuring, representing and visualizing the scope is the EAP (Project Analytical Framework).

For Junior Oak (2012, p. 249)

"Scope management consists in keeping the project within the limits for which it was created, according to a quality of services and products generated. To this end, it is recommended to adopt systematic scope planning on a specific scope management basis, as well as to define the analytical structure of the project (EAP)".

The EAP is a subdivision of the main project deliveries into smaller and more easily manageable units called deliverables.

Fig. 54 - deliverables
Source: freepik (2020)

Deliverables are documents, prototypes and all intangibles (such as training and homologation) that the project must deliver when it is completed. We can compare deliverables, such as rapid product delivery to customers (Fig.54).

For Cierco et. al. (2012), the EAP is based on project content and input generated through the knowledge of project managers and experts who have experienced similar projects. It is organized in a hierarchical manner, and in its graphic form is like an organizational chart.

Cruz (2013,p.121) comments that "the EAP allows the team to have a visual follow-up of all the objects that need to be built and their hierarchical distribution [...] allows the team [...] not to leave any incomplete work packages". For Xavier (2008, p.24), the components at the lowest levels of the Analytical Project Framework (those that have not been decomposed and there is no need for decomposition) are called work packages or deliverables, and are the logical basis for defining activities, assigning activities, estimating costs, and execution time.

An example of the CAS is illustrated in Fig. 55 below, with four levels, the first level corresponding to the project name; the second level corresponding to the project life cycle (management stage and stages or phases of project execution and closure); and the third level corresponding to sub-levels of planning and monitoring and control within project management. The third and fourth levels also include the definition of deliverables or work packages, where the scope, time and cost of the project will be determined.

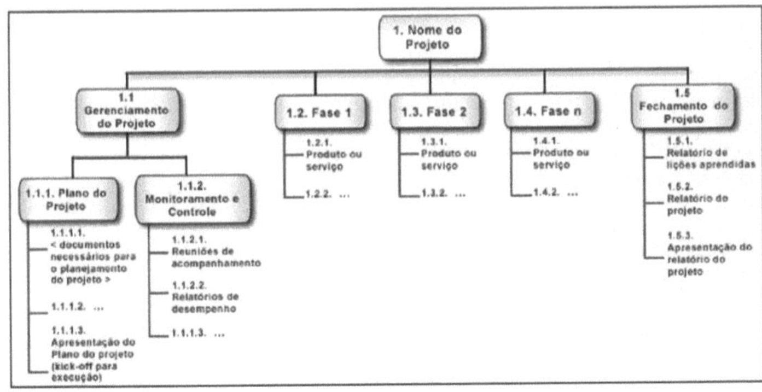

Fig. 55 - EAP Model - Project Analytical Structure.

Source: Xavier (2008, p.22).

For Heldman (2006, p.125) , "there is no "right" way to build the CAS. In practice the tree structure (which resembles an organogram) is used frequently, but it is also possible to compose a PAE schematically [... with another type of diagram]". The PAE can be represented through a *Mind Map* (Fig.56), or a tree with branches (sublevels) and practiced in the *PM Mind Map* method, or through topics and subtopics, representing levels and sublevels, and can be built in a spreadsheet.

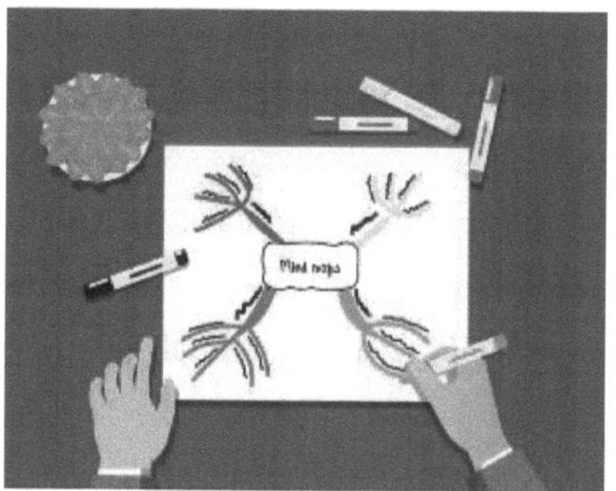

Fig. 56 - Mind Map - representation of a mental map
Source: freepik / freehahn_vect (2020)

For Martins (2007, p.66) regardless of the type of project the construction of the WBS (EAP) should not emphasize the sequence of tasks. The objective is to identify the packages, preparing a *checklist* for the definition of all the activities that will be performed in the construction of the product. This is a fact, because the sequence of activities must be carried out through specific methods of prioritisation and sequencing.

Martins (2007, p.67), comments on some characteristics of WBS:

●É always assembled based on product and project scope;

●É based on WBS that all project elements are planned: scope, time, cost, quality, human resources, communication, risk and procurement.

●O WBS, starts with the breakdown of the project into sub-projects, and these into new sub-projects, successively until the last level is identified.

●O work package is the lowest level of project management.

The EAP or WBS and *Mind Map* are tools to represent and visualize the scope dimension, however it is possible to add the time, cost and human resources of the activity to be executed, as additional information. The smaller the deliverable work package, the more efficient its control will be, that is, the more control the manager will have. of what should be done, in how much time it should be done, who will do it and how much the deliverable work will cost.

The next step within the planning process is to dimension, in detail, how the time management of a project will be performed. In hand we have only the scope and by caution, the previous time of the project and activities, through the *Project Charter* and the EAP.

2.4.5 Time management of a project

Time management in relation to deliverables is related to the scope "what to deliver?" and "when to deliver?". After defining the activities and work packages, it is necessary to dimension the time or periods of deliveries, already specified, previously in the EAP (Project Analytical Structure) or through other project activity decomposition diagrams, such as *PM Mind Map*. For this it is necessary to check again the activities and the main documents to plan and manage the project time.

Chart 22 presents the activities for time planning: elaboration of the time management plan, identification of activities, sequencing of activities, estimation of resources and durations for activities. The artifacts generated by the time planning activities are: time management plan and schedule.

Table 22 - Activity and documents in time planning.

Time planning activities	
Drawing up the time management plan	Time Management Plan
Identify activities	Schedule
Sequencing activities	
Estimate resources for activities	
Estimate durations for activities	

Source: Camargo (2018, p.105).

It is possible to visualise the scope and time management processes, as well as the sequence after the creation of the EAP and the development of the project activities schedule through the diagram in Fig. 57. The time management plan contains the activities: identifying the activities, sequencing the activities, estimating resources for the activities and estimating durations for the activities, thus generating the schedule artifact. Note that for the execution of time management activities it is necessary to enter the EAP (Project Analytical Framework) artefact.

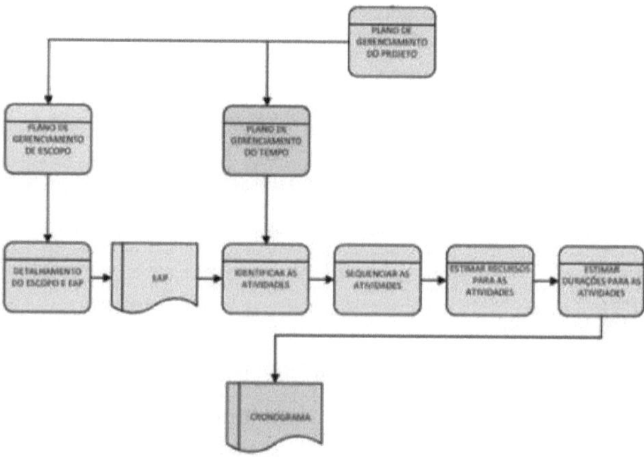

Fig. 57 - Scope and time management processes - after the construction of the EAP a schedule of programme activities is developed

We see in the diagram in Fig. 57 that the management of the time plan, depends on the elaboration of the scope management plan. The scope and time processes are integrated through inputs and outputs of each process in the project life cycle. Any change in scope must be adjusted immediately to all the artefacts of the integrated processes, as they systematically reflect the project as a whole. If the customer requests a new requirement in the course of the project life cycle, the scope, time and cost must be rescaled. Not that this is impossible to achieve, but the closer the changes are to the implementation stage, the greater the impact on the project, and rework must be carried out. Carvalho and Rabechini Jr (2009, p.146), "presents a template for the definition of activities" in EAP, Box 23. It requires information on the scope of the project plan and Project Charter, such as work package, activity level, client, project, name of activity, responsible, description of the activity, inputs, resources and outputs.

Table 23 - Template for activity definition

Work Package - Activity Level
Client:
Projects:
Activity:
Responsible:
Description:
Start:
Ending:
Entries:
Resources:
Exits:

Source: adapted from Carvalho and Rabechini Jr (2009, p.146).

To understand the inputs and outputs of the activity (work package, lower manageable level), we must remember the concept of processes. A process can contain sub-processes and these in activities or tasks, and these can be further subdivided into routines and work instructions. The smallest manageable unit is a task that consists of a work instruction.

Fig. 58 shows an example of PAE, with its tasks, subtasks and work packages (deliverable). For example, task 1.1 (level 2) is broken down into subtasks, 1.1.2, 1.1.3, 1.1.n. and subtask 1.1.2 (level 3) is broken down into work packages (last activity level - level 4), 1.1.1.1, 1.1.1.2, ...1.1.1.n.

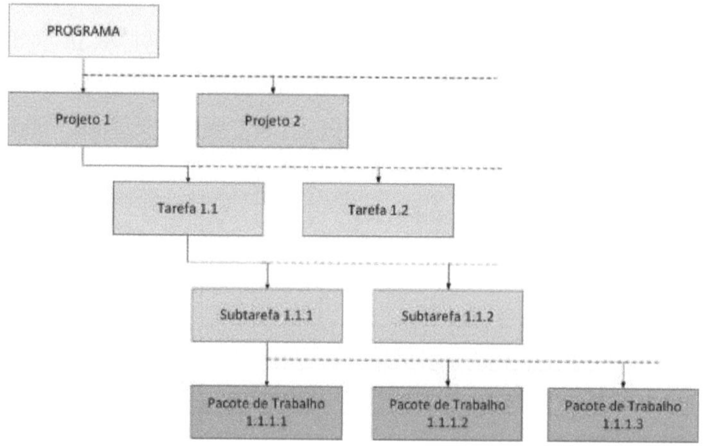

Fig. 58 - Example of EAP.

Jacobs and Chase (2012, p. 320) explain that a task is a subdivision added to the project. It often lasts no longer than a few months and is carried out by a group or organisation. A subtask or routine can be used if it is necessary to subdivide the project into more significant parts. The work package, on the other hand, is a set of activities that are already at their most divisible. The work package provides a description of what is to be done according to Box 21 (suggested template), description of the activity, inputs, outputs, resources, persons responsible, etc., when the work is to start and finish, the budget, performance measures and specific events to be achieved at a certain point in time. Each EAP/WBS activity or work package will have its scope, time and individual activity sizing. The highest level (level 0) will have the time and cost of the sub-activities (the other levels 1 to 4), and the activities at level 4 will be the final breakdown of project activity.

We have seen that the CAS or other diagram that breaks down the activity to make it better manageable, is a necessary artifact for the construction of the schedule. Besides defining what will be done, how it will be done, it is vital to define when it will be done. Now let's look at the notion of when the activity will be carried out by planning the sequencing of project activities.

For Martins (2007,p.71), "after the definitions of the activities, the next step in time planning is to sequence the activities. The result is the [...] [Fig. 59, for the WBS work packages] network".

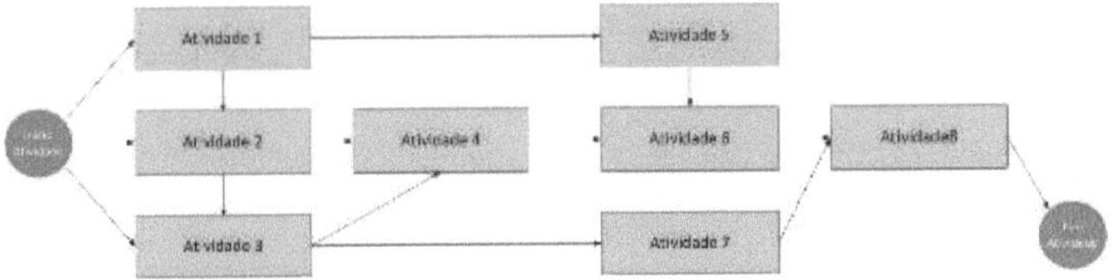

Fig. 59 - Network Diagram.

According to PMI (2004) apud Carvalho and Rabechini Jr. (2009, p.147), the process of sequencing activities "makes it possible to identify and document the relationships of dependencies between activities. For Maximiano (2010,p.89), "the sequencing allows to establish the priorities and then graphically represent the relationships and the chain of activities, summarized in a diagram of precedence. Also called PDM - *Proceding Diagramming*

Method, which represents the activities by us, rectangles and the relations of dependencies, the arrows (Fig. 56). It is used by most project management software.

Maximiano (2010, p.91) summarizes in a table of precedence where the activities of the CAS are listed, Box 24. The activities are entered randomly in the table. This table corresponds to the diagram (PLE) Fig. 58 (work packages - last level activities - level 4 in the example).

Table 24 - Precedences, which indicates the sequencing of activities.

Number	Activity	Duration	Previous activity
1	Work Package 1	1 day	None on the list
2	Work Package 4	1 week	None on the list
3	Work Package 2	1 week	1,3
4	Work Package 5	1 week	2
5	Work Package 6	1 day	4,3
6	Work Package 3	1 day	None on the list
7	Work Package 7	1 day	6

Source: adapted from Maximiano (2010, p.91).

Following the time management planning process, after the sequencing of activities a chart is drawn (precedence diagram) Fig. 60.

> "In the precedence diagram, [...] each activity is represented by a 'node' - a symbol (usually a rectangle or circle) within which the letter or number designating the activity or describing the activity is written down, the arrows represent the relationship of dependency and the sequence of activities" (MAXIMIANO, 2010, p.92).

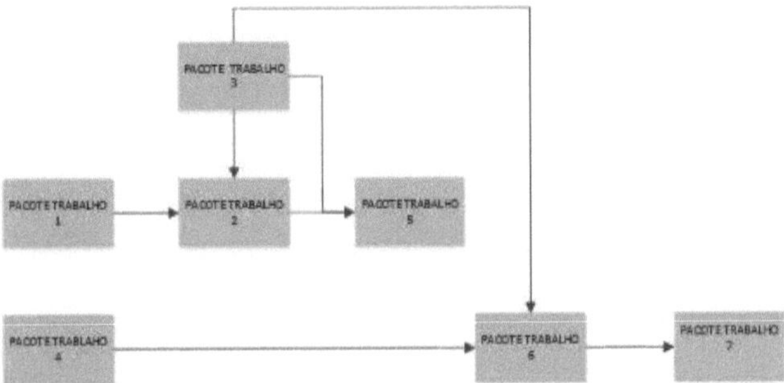

Fig. 60 - Diagram of precedence of Table 22.

The 'sequence table' and 'precedence diagram' artefacts support the manager and the project team in constructing the timeline artefact, which can be either complete, containing the sequencing of activities, the dependencies, and execution time, or in a compact form.

According to Maximiano (2010, p.94) "the next step in the planning process is to decide when the activities take place and draw up a schedule. The schedule is a graph that shows the distribution of activities over a calendar". The schedule is based on the estimation of the duration (term) and resources (people and materials) and cost of the activities.

Remember that in Table 24 and Fig. 60 at the time of defining the activities, the beginning and end (duration), costs, entrances and exits of the activity were already foreseen. However, a review of this information should be carried out in the development of the schedule. The estimates of duration of activities (programming) are performed by techniques, as suggested by Carvalho and Rabechini Jr. (2009, p.152):

- Gráfico from Gantt [Bars].
- Critical Path Method (CPM).
- Program Evaluation & Review Technique (PERT).

"The Gantt [Bars] chart consists of bars drawn within a calendar, which represent the periods for the realisation of a project's activities" (MAXIMIANO, 2010, p.101). For Daychoum (2005,p.46), the Gantt chart allows the visualisation of the activities in execution and those that do not have a break, called critical path. An example of a Gantt chart (activities or projects x time) is shown in Fig. 61.

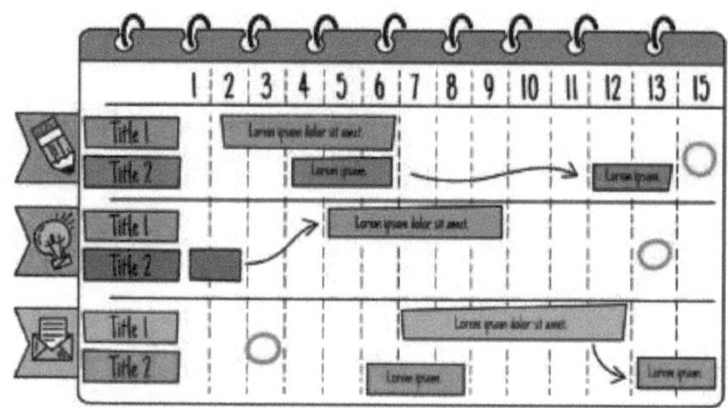

Fig. 61 - Gantt chart
Source: freepik (2020)

PERT-CPM is one of the most complex of all types of schedules. It is often used in larger and more complex projects that require a more rigid compliance of time and cost of each task or routine. An important analysis in programming, that of the critical path, which aims to define the minimum duration of the project. For Maximiano (2010, p. 96) "the critical path is the longest path from the first to the last activity of a project - the one in which the activities have the longest duration".

PERT and CPM are two similar methods or techniques, PERT uses a more complex stochastic system (statistical model) based on three predictions that are applied to determine the most likely date for project completion. The

CMP adopts only the estimated duration of the activities (MAXIMIANO, 2010).

An example of a PERT/CPM network is shown in Table 25 and Figure 59, with activity dependencies and duration in days. For example, activity "A" has a duration of 2 days. Activity "B" has a duration of 3 days. Activity A is not dependent on any activity. Activity B depends on activity A and so on for the other activities.

Chart 25 - Table of activities with dependencies and duration in days.

Activities		Dependency	Duration (in days)
A	Make an inventory of the section material per job	-	2
B	Crate the material	A	3
C	Transfer boxed material	B	4
D	Tidying up the floor of the new site	-	4
E	Painting walls of the new site	D	7
F	Adequate electrical installations of the new site.	D	3
G	Install new site lighting	F	2
H	Assembling furniture in the new location	E, G	6
I	Dismembering the material	C, H	2
J	Allocate the material	J	1

Source: Muniz Junior et. al (2012,p.63).

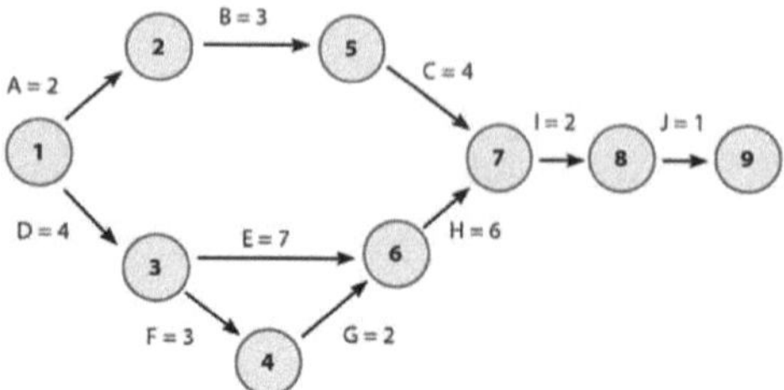

Fig. 62 - PERT/CPM network that shows the activity, the duration in days and the sequences.
Source: Muniz Junior et. al (2012,p.63).

MUNIZ JUNIOR (2012, p.63) comments that the minimum duration, [in this example of Fig. 62] is 20 days, because the path 1-3-6-7-8-9 [critical path] is the longest. Any delay in the critical path tasks will cause a delay in the implementation of the project as a whole.

2.4.6 Managing the cost of a project

Continuing the sizing of activities resources, cost is one of the important elements that must be integrated in time and scope, when you have more resources, the term decreases and the cost increases. When you redefine the scope, greater or lesser, it will be the time and cost of the project. Fig.63 illustrates calculation activity for budgeting, which is vital in project management.

Fig. 63 - budgeting activity

Source: lovelayday12 (2020)

Maximiano (2010, p. 107) comments that each of the resources of the related, sequenced, and dimensioned activities at the definition stage has a unit cost. For example, the hour worked by an employee of a legal analyst is equal to the employee's total monthly cost (including social charges, benefits and other costs) divided by the average number of hours worked per month.

Regarding the Martins budgeting process (2007, p.76), "it aggregates the estimated costs of [EAP]/WBS items to establish a baseline of total project costs. The scope statement provides a summary budget, while the budget presents the details".

Camargo (2014, p.111) presents in Table 26 the activities and documents in cost planning. In the activities of defining the procedures for surveying and controlling costs, and in drawing up the budget, the artifacts "Cost Management Plan", "cost estimates" and "budget" are generated.

Table 26 - activities and documents in cost planning.

Activities to plan costs	Documents generated

141

Define survey procedures and cost control	Cost Management Plan
Estimate project costs	Cost estimates
Drawing up the project budget	Budget

Source: Camargo (2014, p. 111).

The cost estimates and budget are generated from the cost management plan. The cost management plan must be documented in accordance with Table 27: "In managing project costs we are concerned with the preparation and control of the project budget, in aggregate and not activity by activity, managing the factors that may influence it and deviate from those desired" (Carvalho and Rabechini Jr., 2009, p.174).

Table 27 - project cost management plan document

Documents
Project Title
Name of the person drawing up the document
Description of cost management processes (general rules)
Description of the management reserves and the autonomy of their use
Cost change control system
Frequency of evaluation of project budget and management reserves
Financial allocation of budget changes
Name of the person responsible for the plan
Frequency of cost management plan update
Other issues related to cost management not foreseen in the plan
recording of document changes
approvals

Source: Vargas (2016, p.86)

After checking the correct time to carry out the project cost planning and defining what the documents and other cost plan artifacts are, it is necessary to detail what these artifacts are. We will now see about a project cost forecast.

For Camargo (2014, p.111-112) "the way in which costs are stipulated and managed will depend on the type of project and the power that the project manager has to create cost estimates and close the project budget.
Some guidelines for cost estimation divided into 4 steps:

- prepare a cost estimate;
- draw up a detailed budget;
- to improve the budget while work is being carried out and the recurring costs during the course of the project; see below for more details.

If the project leader receives a fixed amount for the project budget in this case budgeting from the strategies of the business budget plan, the planning of the scope and other areas of knowledge of the project will revolve around this amount. The value will serve as the general constraint for all project decisions.

If the project does not have a pre-fixed value, or if the value is capable of being negotiated, the cost management of the project will cover four basic steps: 1st step is to prepare a cost estimate with an order of magnitude from -50% to +100% in the initial phase of the project initial cost estimate in the Project Charter, the 2nd step is to prepare a detailed budget with an order of magnitude from -10% to + 15%, served by the cost analysis of all project activities and obtaining conventional approval of the value. Step 3 is to improve the budget while the work is carried out and the recurring costs during the course of the project. At the end of this stage, the figures should be in the range of 5 to 10% above or below the budgeted amount for the project. In step 4, the budget is to be monitored and controlled over the course of the project tasks.

To start the process of preparing the project budget, the second step is related to good estimates, and there are several ways to make these cost estimates in projects, the most common are: top-down, bottom-down, parametric, direct costs, indirect costs, fixed costs and variable costs:

a) Direct costs: these are those costs that are diversified according to their effective applications, such as labour, materials and direct expenditures (CARVALHO and RABECHINI JR., 2009, p.181).

b) Indirect Costs: these costs are not diversified according to their effective applications and are distributed and divided by applying the EAP account system, such as indirect materials, indirect labor (specialized quality audit personnel, project support teams, among others) (CARVALHO and RABECHINI JR., 2009, p.181). Indirect costs are related to project activities, e.g. electricity, telephone, water or internet expenses.

c) Top-down or top-down: it is related to previous projects and to more common costs. Also called forecast by analogy is based on information from projects that have already been carried out, on the outcome of equivalent projects, it is usually used in the first phase of the project, when there is not enough knowledge for more precise estimates (MONTEIRO, 2008,p.111).

d) Bottom-Up: "is the most complete and accurate estimate. From the breakdown we arrive at the maximum detail of the activities, clearly identifying how much time is needed to do them, as well as the type of resources required [...] and the cost of each activity and project" (MONTEIRO, 2008, p. 112). It is therefore possible to remember the breakdown of activities by EAP/WBS, where each activity is the maximum breakdown (last level EAP work package, with its respective cost.

e)   Parametric: "in which the statistical relationship between historical data and other variables (e.g. [...] lines of code in software development) is used to calculate the estimate" (CAMARGO, 2018, p.111).

f)   Fixed cost: costs that do not depend on the quantity manufactured: they can be rent, cleaning, security, insurance, marketing and other services independent from production.

g)   Variable costs: costs that vary according to the tasks performed for the project, specifically for the project as hourly/employee of temporary workers hired to carry out tests on a specific project component or monthly rent of facilities allocated to part of the project.

Therefore time and cost management are essential within a project's life cycle. It is necessary to understand that it is also necessary to manage the software development process through efficient planning, monitoring and control. It is from the execution of metrics that the software process can achieve the desired and necessary quality. We will understand better the concepts of metrics and software measurements.

2.5 Software Metrics

In order to understand about the estimates by function points and points by case of use in a software, it is necessary to understand the concepts of measurement, metrics and indicators in process and software design. For Sommerville (2011, p.465-466) software measurement is used in place of revisions to make judgments about software quality. If the software reaches a quality starting point, then it is approved without revision. A software metric is a feature of a software system, system documentation or development process that can be measured. Examples of these measurements include the size of a product in lines of code, the number of defects reported in a software product delivered, or the number of man-hours (effort) to develop a system component. Software metrics can be control metrics, which refer to management, or they can also be forecast metrics, helping to estimate the effort required to make changes to the software.

In a software process and software design the measurement, or measurement system, is essential for the management decision making of all stages of software development and the scope, time and cost of the project, i.e. to manage it is necessary to measure. Sommerville (2011, p.466) "comments that control and forecast metrics can influence management decision making. Managers use process metrics to decide whether changes should be made to the process".

Fig. 64 below illustrates a set of indicators (a measurement system). Each indicator has a minimum or maximum target or threshold.

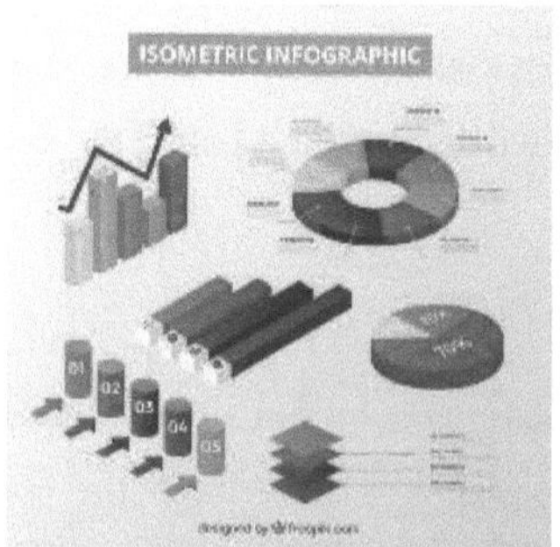

Fig. 64 - Set of indicators
Source: freepik (2020)

Metrics, therefore, would be measured, values collected during a software process or design (Fig.65). The software project manager can use indicators to control the costs, scopes and time of a project or predict possible risks that might occur. A Software Engineer can control the required metrics for coding software requirements, or the required performance that the software needs to achieve, or even if error metrics are outside of the acceptable standard.

Fig. 65 - Metric - value collected during a process

Source: freepik / iconicbestiary (2020)

For Pressman and Maxim (2016) there are metrics or measures in the process and project domain. Process metrics are collected in all projects and over long periods. The result of this set of information, during this period, provides process indicators that lead to the improvement of the software process. The project metrics allow the software project manager to evaluate the status of an ongoing project before critical situations come to light (forecast and control metrics). With this predictability he can track risks, adjust workflows, evaluate the project team's ability to quality control software artifacts. To make clear the difference between the concepts of Measurement, Metrics and Indicators, let's look at the concept of each one:

Measure: it is the whole, association of a numerical quantity to a characteristic. Ex: How many customers have bought the product? How many lines of code does the program have?

Fig. 66 - Metric - quantity of a task or procedure performed at a given time
Source: freepik / stories (2020)

Metric: is the set of measures defined over time, using the same measuring method. Ex during the semester, how many lines of code are written? During the month, how much was the development cost (Fig.66).

Indicator: is a measurement variable or metric with respect to a benchmark. It is usually represented as a percentage (%). Example: number of customers/number of orders, number of lines of code/time etc.

2.5.1 Software measurement process

The collection of process data from software projects (measurements), over time (metrics), forming a measurement system (set of indicators) can be illustrated by the following diagram (Fig. 67).

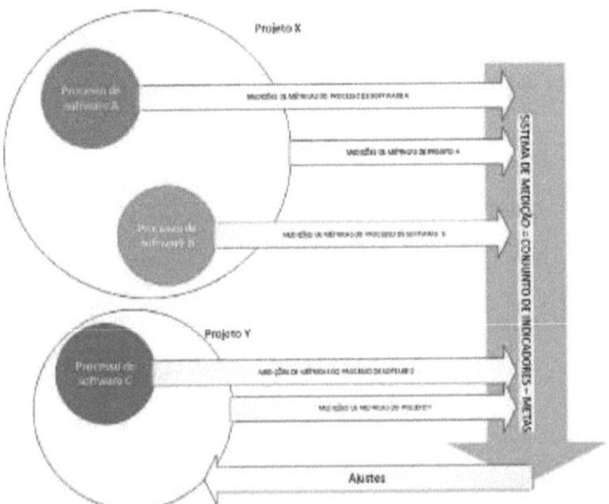

Fig. 67 - Cycle of continuous improvement of processes and software projects

Through these indicators and an acceptable target, it is expected that the measures collected will also be acceptable, i.e. consistent with an internal or external standard. A standardised average is always sought in processes and projects. For example, that the number of defects does not exceed 10 or that the number of lines of code in software development does not exceed 100. As if it were a measurement gauge to be followed in the processes. However, a measurement or metric can inform good things (conformities) and bad things (non-conformities) in a process. If there are non-conformities, then the process should be improved or even the ideal "supposed" metric or measure improved.

You see in Fig. 67, that there is a cycle of continuous improvement in the measurement process. This occurs when the measurements/metrics or process/project adjustments are made.

An important metric within the software process are size oriented metrics. For Pressman (2016, p.709) "they are created by quality and/or productivity standardization, taking into account the size of the software produced". This size oriented software metric can be presented in various ways. Sommerville (2011, p.469) presents these metric shapes:

- Fan-in/Fan-out:
    - Fan-in is a measure of the number of functions or methods that call other functions or methods (function of x).
    - Metrics are called function points.
    - Fan-out is the number of functions that are called by the function of x.
- Code length:
    - This is a measure of the size of a programme.
    - The larger the code the more prone the software is to errors.
- Cyclomatic complexity:
    - It is a measure of programme control complexity and is related to the comprehensibility of the programme
- Length of identifiers:
    - It is a measure of the average length of identifiers such as names of variables, classes, methods etc. in a programme.
    - The longer the identifiers, the more understandable it is and with this the cyclomatic complexity decreases.
    - related to the comprehensibility of the programme.
- Depth of conditional nesting:
    - It is a measure of depth of nesting statements if in a programme.
- Fog. Index
    - It is a measure of average length of words and sentences in documents.

Within the size metrics the function point and use cases metrics stand out. Let's look at the concepts of the function point metric. According to Pressman (2016, p.659)

> "Function point (FP) metrics can be a means of measuring the functionality provided by a system. Using historical data, FP metrics can be employed to (1) estimate the cost or work required to design, code and test the software. (2) predict the number of errors that will be found during testing; and (3) predict the number of components and/or number of lines projected from source code in the implemented system".

The function point metric is derived from a relationship between (1) direct calculable measures of the software information domain (functional elements) and (2) qualitative assessments of the software complexity (weight factor: simple, medium or complex). The values of the information domains or functional elements are defined according to Table 28 below:

Table 28 - Description of the information areas or functional elements.

Information domains or Functional Elements	Description
Number of external entries (Here - *internal inputs*)	Input of user data or transmitted from another application (logical transactions). They enter the application and keep the internal data. Example: data input fields.
Number of external outputs (EOs - *external outputs*)	Data output. Provide data to users. These are logical transactions where data leaves the application to provide information to users. Example: reports, screens, error messages.
Number of external consultations (EQs - *external inquiries*)	It is defined as an online entry that results in an immediate online response from the software. These are logical transactions where an entry requests a response from the application.
Number of internal logical files (ILFs - *Internal lógical files*)	Each internal logical file is a logical grouping of data that resides within the boundaries of the application and is maintained through internal and external

	entries. Logical grouping of data maintained by the application.
Number of external interface files (EIFs - *external interface files*)	Each external interface file is a logical grouping of data that resides outside the application, but provides data that can be used by the application. Logical grouping of data referenced by the application, but maintained by another application.

Source: adapted from Pressman (2016, p.659-660)

An example of function points calculation is given by table 1 below, multiplying the count by the information domain by the weight factor. The example considers that the information domains are of simple level. Depending on the project, the weights for each value of the domain can be defined according to specific criteria or called dependent functions.

Table 1 - Calculation of function points

Value of the information domain	Counting	Weight Factor			Total (function size
		Simple	Average	Complex	
EIs	3	x 3	4	6	= 9
EOs	2	x 4	5	3	= 8
EQs	2	x 3	6	5	= 6
EIFs	1	x 7	2	1	= 7
ILFs	4	x 5	8	5	= 20
				Total Count	= 50

The result of the total count is the sum of all the software's function points. The weight factor depends on several factors with specific criteria such as user importance, intensity of use, interface and complexity and uniformity. They have this denomination due to the degree of dependence they have on correlated functions. These dependent function factors are part of the result formula. Let's look at the factors that can form the weight factor:

o Importance of the User: it is the degree of importance that the user gives to the function. This degree can be collected in interviews and meetings with the user. It can be of low, normal and high level.

o Intensity of use: is the degree of use of functions in a time interval. There are functions that are used more often and functions that are used less often in a given interval or period.

o Interface: measures the degree of interrelationship between files (affected by functions) and measured functions (functions that affect files). The interface criteria is related to the number of changes and the number of files accessed by the

o Complexity: is the degree of complexity of the function given by its algorithm (program that executes the function). This is measured by the amount of if or Case condition command of the algorithm.

The formula for calculating the dependent functions is given by:

FD = ((Importance of the user + Intensity of use + Interface + Complexity) / 20) x Uniformity.

When the paradigm used in the software development process is object orientation, points per use case (PCU, based strongly on UML (*Unified Modeling Language*). The use case estimate, according to Pressman and Maxim (2016, 740-742) provides information on the software scope and requirements to the software team. Once the use cases have been prepared they can be used to estimate the size of the software. The use case represents a discrete task involving external interaction with a system. In its simplest form, a use case is shown as an ellipse, with the actors involved represented by stick figures. Usage case diagrams give a simple overview of an interaction (SOMMERVILLE, 2011, p.86-87).

This method of size estimation is given by "use case points" (PCU) and consists of relating and counting the actors, use cases and transactions, and performing the weighting (classification) of the technical and environmental complexity of each component.

Table 29 - Complexity and weight related to each actor

Complexity	Description	Weight
Simple Actor	System accessed through a programming API (Application Programming Interface)	1
Middle Actor	Applications based on protocols or by command lines. Ex.: TCP/IP	2
Complex Actor	User interacting through a graphic interface (*stand-alone* or Web)	3

Table 29 above informs the weight to be given to each actor according to their complexity related to user access, either by a graphical interface, web for example, of maximum weight (3), or by a transmission by protocols, TCP/IP for example, of intermediate weight (2) or by access by APIs (Application Programming interface), of low weight (1). After the weight for each actor is assigned, all values are added together. This total is called Total Unadjusted Weights of Actors (TPNAA). It is also possible to consider instead of user-interface interaction, the number of Database entities involved, with or without complex business rules. Another factor that should be considered in the PCU metric is with respect to the "Use Case" elements. From a requirements gathering document, the use case diagram and the class diagram the transactions of the software and the classes of each use case are performed. In this factor is considered the number of transactions including alternative flows, and the "transaction" is an event between the actor and the system.

Table 30 below shows the weights given according to the number of transactions criterion.

Table 30 - Complexity and Weight according to the complexity of the transaction.

Complexity	Description	Weight
Simple	Consider up to 3 transactions with 5 less classes of analysis and including alternative flow.	5
Average	Consider 4 to 7 transactions with 5 to 10 classes of analysis and including alternative flow.	10
Complex	Consider from 8 transactions with at least 10 classes and including alternative flow	15

After relating the use cases and attributing it to a degree of complexity, according to the table above, being simple, average and complex the respective complexities, the total unadjusted use case weights (TPNAUC) are calculated. After determining the TPNAA and the TPNAUC, both unadjusted totals of the actors and use cases are added together:

$$\sum TPNA = TPNAA + TPNAUC$$

After that, the factors adjusted through technical and environmental complexity must be calculated. The technical complexity has a value of variation between 0 and 5, where 0 has no degree of difficulty in building the system. The value 5 has a high degree of difficulty in constructing the system.

Technical factors are multiplied by weights that can be:

- o Application performance: this factor has a weight of 1 and corresponds to factors meeting the functional and non-functional requirements of the application.

- o Complex internal processing: this factor has a weight of 1 and corresponds to factors of complexity of the algorithm with respect to its processing.

- o Reusability of code in other applications: This factor has a weight of 1.0 and corresponds to modularization through functions procedures in the reuse of these routines or libraries in other applications.

- o Ease of installation: This factor has a weight of 0.5 and corresponds to the ease of installation of the software on computers, such as simplicity, easy understanding and with a minimum of additional requirements (need libraries or pre-installed programs).
- o Portability: this factor has a weight of 2.0 which corresponds to the operation of the application on various equipment and platforms.

After summing up the weights of technical complexity through the sum $FCT = 1.4 + (-0.03 * \sum TPCT * \sum Fator)$. Remembering that the factor varies from 0 to 5.

After determining the technical value, the environmental complexity factor must be evaluated. This factor is related to the skills and competences of the professionals. This value varies between 0 and 5, the zero value indicates zero skills and abilities and 5 indicates high skill and competence of professionals. These factors are:

- o Factor of familiarity with the software development process: this factor weighs 1.5 and is related to the knowledge and experience with the phases and activities of the software process.
- o Application Experience Factor: this factor has a weight of 0.5 and is related to the experience regarding the specific application developed.
- o Object Oriented Experience Factor: This factor has weight 1 and is related to experience with programming languages and object oriented development (OO) techniques.

- o Leadership ability factor: this factor weighs 0.5 and is related to leadership ability with the software project team.
- o Motivation Factor: this factor has weight 1, and is related to the motivation of the software development team.
- o Stable Requirements Factor: this factor weighs 1.0 and is related to the minimum change in requirements during the software life cycle.
- o Partial dedication factor: this factor has weight -1 and is related to the time of dedication to the software development process.
- o Programming Language Difficulty Factor: this factor weighs -1.0 and is related to insufficient or no competence in the programming languages used in the software process.

The formula for calculating environmental complexity is given by FCA $= 1.4 + (-0.03 * \sum TPCA * \sum$ of environmental factors). The total calculation of adjusted Use Case points is given by PUCA = TPNA x TPCT X FCA.

We can conclude that when we use the software size estimation per function point, this is applied in programming paradigms that use function and procedures. Use Case Point Estimation is applied to programming paradigms and object oriented specifications expressed in Use Case, such as Java language and UML modeling. The disadvantages in Use Case Point Estimation is that the method cannot be used before the analysis of project requirements is performed. In order for the metric not to become subjective, there must be a pattern defined in the modeling in the processes and software projects, in this case UML is indicated. From the estimates we have studied, by function points and Use Case points, it is possible to calculate the duration and cost of the project from the effort estimate. The cost and time estimates are linked to the effort released from the estimate made from the function points or by Use Case points.

We have seen that software metrics are essential procedures within a software development process. However, it is necessary to understand that in addition to tools, methods and techniques, or project approaches, it is necessary to know the importance of people and their relationships within a software project. Let us now look at the communication management process and the relationships of influence that occur between those involved within a project.

2.6 People and communication management

Fig. 68 - Communication of People in Projects
Source: freepik / stories (2020)

The project manager must take responsibility for the project, ensuring that the result will be achieved and answer for the consequences. He must be a good planner, organiser, people manager, interface manager, technology manager, implementer, communications mediator (Fig.68), and method formulator. However, the leader must influence and lead people towards the achievement of the project goals. Maximiano (2010) comments that leadership is an ability that develops (and turns into a skill), through training and experience, and an attitude - some people have more skill and a favourable attitude to leadership than others. However, project leaders can build different styles. For Carvalho Junior (2012, p.43) "each project manager has a leadership style. This style will be followed by the project team [...], the manager must adapt to the various styles and work with it". Regardless of the style, the leader, and the whole team, must be receptive and communicative. Communication is vital with all those involved and interested in the project. The task oriented style characterises the behaviour of managers who concentrate on themselves the authority and decision-making process, emphasising the results of the project. The people-oriented style is characterised by managers who emphasise the team's participation in the decision-making process and the human climate of the project (MAXIMIANO, 2010) is the case in Fig. 69.

Fig. 69 - Team work
Source: freepik / studiogstock (2020)

As the two previous styles are not exclusive, leaders can combine the varying degrees of team involvement in the decision-making process. The situation-oriented style becomes effective depending on the situation in which the project manager is faced. Other styles can be developed such as charismatic and transactional leadership.

According to Maximiano (2010, p.275), he presents these leaderships that involve material rewards and moral rewards. Charismatic leadership has characteristics:

-Style   that has a team-oriented focus on the project's mission and offers symbolic psychological rewards.

The transactional leadership has characteristics:

-It identifies   the personal and calculating interests of the team, cultivating material reward performance.

In short, the best leadership is the situational one based on the team's motivation and combined skills. Maximiano (2010, p.273) comments that when there is a low motivation and competence in the team an emphasis is needed on all leadership functions such as training, encouragement, personal counselling, performance monitoring and verification of results. When team motivation is high but competence is low, i.e. the team has a positive pre-disposition in the project, however it has a lack of qualification, it is necessary to emphasise the leadership function to provide training, guidance and feedback. When motivation is low and qualification is high, the team may need personal attention, encouragement and possibly some kind of incentive.

Another issue that must be taken into consideration in relation to the management of the team and other stakeholders is the understanding of the relationships between them. Stakeholders are people, groups of people or entities that participate and/or influence, directly and indirectly, with interests in their evolution or when they are reached by their results (ORTH, 2006, cited by NORO, 2012). Managing stakeholders is about managing a power of influence in relationships and managing conflicts in those relationships. Power is the power that can impose on the other party in a relationship. Power of influence has a regulatory, coercive and utilitarian function in a process of decision making and achievement of objectives in a project.

Before we look at what these influences are on the decision-making process and achievement of project objectives, let us look at the main roles of the stakeholders in box 31 below.

Table 31 - The main stakeholders and their description

Key Stakeholders	Description
Project Manager	Individual responsible for project management;
Client/user	Person or organisation who will use the product of the project, there may be several levels of customers/users;
Implementing organisation	Company whose employees are directly involved in the execution of the project work;
Project Team Members	Group that is carrying out the project work;
Project management team	People from the project team who are directly involved in project management activities;
Sponsor	People or groups who contribute financial resources, in cash or in kind, to the project.
PMO (Project Management Office)	If it exists within the implementing organisation, it may be an interested party if it has direct or indirect responsibility for the outcome of the project.

Source: PMI (2004) cited by NORO (2012).

Through the graph below "categories of stakeholders" (Fig.7), it illustrates the various influences that occur among stakeholders with characteristics of power, urgency and legitimacy. These influences can occur in isolation or in combination, generating new influences. For example, the combination of 'power' influence with 'legitimacy' influence results in a so-called 'dominant' influence. In the 'dominant' influence relationship, much attention is expected and received from the firm. See that in this relationship of influencing people, there are no urgent actions.

The combination of 'power' influence and 'urgent' influence generates a style of dangerous influences, as this stakeholder possesses a high power and a need for urgency in decision-making and project activities, imposing its will without legitimacy and using force in a coercive or threatening manner. In the case of a combination of 'legitimacy' (legality) and 'urgency' influences are generated as 'dependency', these influences on relationships have the legality of actions and the urgency of planning, implementation and control, but depend on the power of other stakeholders to impose their interests. The power, legitimacy and urgency influences can occur in isolation, as shown in the diagram below (Fig. 70). Power alone becomes a dormant relationship, i.e. it has the power to impose its will (interests) but no legitimacy and urgency. Isolated legitimacy behaves in an arbitrary way. Isolated urgency, on the other hand, as it has no power and no legitimacy, becomes a claimant for decisions and actions of the project.

Fig. 70 - category of stakeholder influences

Source: adapted from Tetrim (2010) apud Noro (2012)

However, all influences can be combined, generating a relationship of influence called 'definitive'. In this case the relationships can occur with all categories of influence according to the interests of the *stakeholders*. In addition to analysing the influences of stakeholders within a project according to their interests, it is possible to analyse the level of authority (power) and grouping the stakeholders, i.e. how much power this group has and its level of concern about the project results. The graph in Fig. 71 below illustrates this relationship.

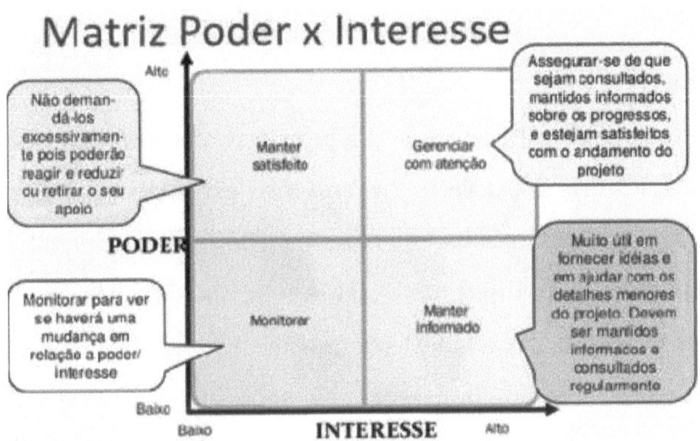

Fig. 71 - power x interest matrix

Source: adapted from PMBOK Guide 5th ed. (2013, p.13).

It is observed that when there is a high power of influence from the leader and a low interest from the team, it is necessary to keep the team satisfied, so that excessive demand can cause it to react, reduce or withdraw its support. If both power and interest influences are low, it is necessary to monitor to see if there is a change in power and/or interest. This management emphasises the monitoring of actions. If the power influence and interests of the team are both high, it is necessary to ensure that the team is informed about progress and that everyone is satisfied with the progress of the project. This is careful management. Finally, we observe in the graph the situation where the power of influence is low, but the interests of the team are high, in which case the leader should direct his expertise to keeping the team informed, providing ideas and consulting regularly.

Another aspect that needs to be understood is the communication process in a project management approach. Faced with this need, when we talk about communication and stakeholders within a project management, in addition to understanding people management and the power of influence between stakeholders, it is vital to comment on the organisational structure where projects occur.

We have seen that the success of a project is related to the best relations and power of influence between the *stakeholders* (power, legitimacy and urgency), as well as their combinations (dormant, arbitrary, claimant, dominant, dependent, dangerous and definitive). However, the projects and resources, which you need (people, machines, equipment), are inserted in an organized structure of work, as shown in Fig. 72. It is in this structure that the communications, interferences and influences between the stakeholders occur. It is in this organisational structure of work that the culture and the way in which employees, employees, analysts, managers and directors exercise, in their functional activities, influences on the way in which the project is conceived, planned, executed and closed.

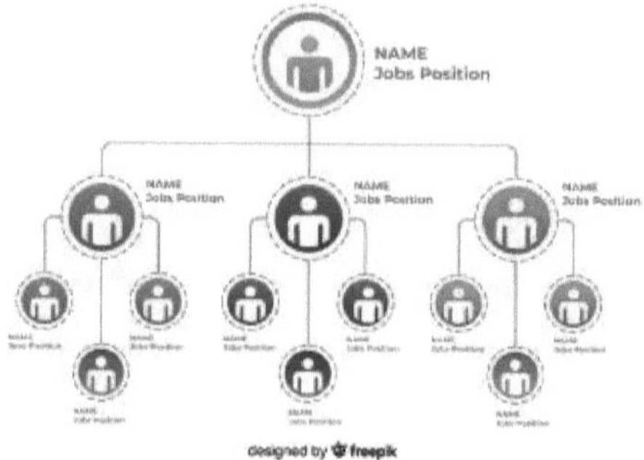

Fig. 72 - organization chart
Source: freepik (2020)

"Some organisations develop a unique culture and style that reflects their value guidelines, internal norms, beliefs and expectations that are reflected in their set of policies, power relations, hierarchical relationships and other factors" (POSSI, 2006, p.22).

Therefore the culture, values, policies, rules, styles and the very work system of an organisation directly influence the projects developed by it. This set of characteristics and ways in which people work in an organization must be aligned with the mission (what the company produces), with the vision (where the company wants to go) of the organization, with the ethical and moral principles, and with the work structure, which determine with the projects will be defined and executed.

With regard to organisational structures, various forms can be designed. The main forms of structures are traditional, projected and matrix. Carvalho and Rabechini Jr (2009, p.25-26), comment that the traditional organizational structure, so called functional, where it is formed by divisions through departments, having greater control, technical domain, less conflict, but due to a diversification of market demand, has become more difficult to manage projects, because in this organizational system tends to meet a departmental point of view and not focused on the client. In order to meet this demand, matrix and projected structures have emerged.

Figs. 73 and 74 illustrate examples of functional and design structure. The Staff that is shown in the structures, correspond to the employees, specialists and support of the area.

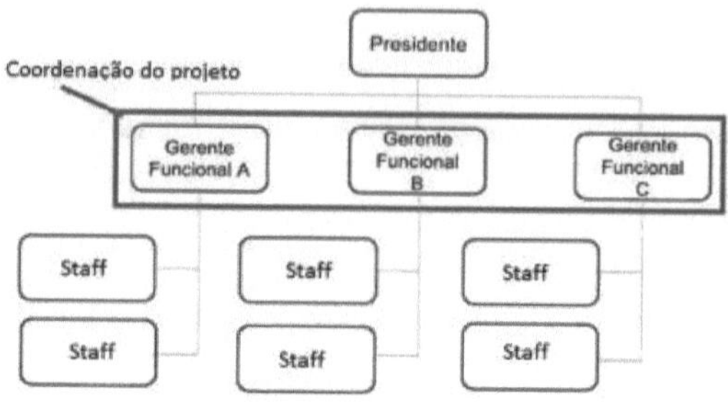

Fig.73 - Functional Structure.

Source: Adapted from Veras (2016, p.75.)

i. Functional Structure: For Possi (2006, p.22), in a functional structure there is greater control of resources (people, equipment, machines), since each employee responds to only one superior, in the case of Fig. 73, "Functional Structure", the employee or Staffs, each has its functional manager (A, B or C). The team members (Staffs) are grouped by specialty (production, marketing, engineering, etc.) and the perceived scope is limited to the boundaries of functions.

It can also be seen that projects are managed by functional managers (A, B and C) and not by specific project managers (independent of the functional area), and departments exert a strong influence on the conduct of projects. Note that the influences of project coordination occur between departments and not between the manager and the Staffs, i.e. the management takes place horizontally in the structure. Often the projects that take place in a functional organisation are not so important in relation to the routine activities of individual departments.

ii. Projected structure: For Possi (2006, p. 23), "companies that organize themselves in a project-oriented manner are project-oriented, i.e. their operation basically consists of the development and execution of projects". According to

Kerzner (2001) the greatest advantage of the project-oriented structure is that a single individual, the project manager, has complete authority over the project as a whole (Fig. 74 - "Project structure").

In the project structure the functional fraction is intrinsic to each project. In this type of organisation the projects are led by the project manager and the functions of the Staffs exist to support the projects.

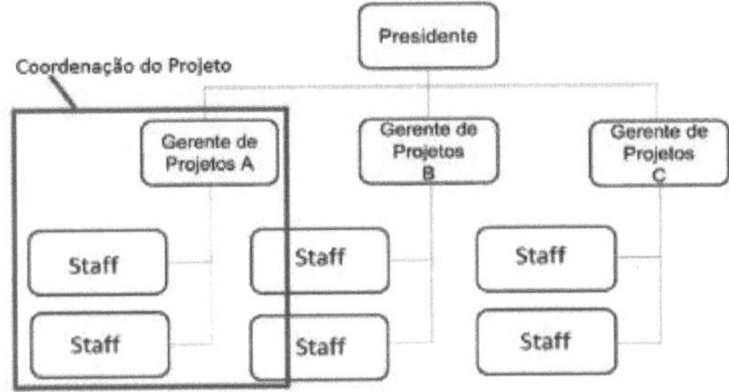

Fig. 74 - Structure by projects.
Source: Adapted from Veras (2016, p.75).

Note in Fig. 74 that the project manager leads a team consisting of Staffs from various areas (marketing, production, engineering etc.). The project is conducted vertically in the structure, where all the support and resources take place through the support of the areas.

iv. Matrix Structure: establishes the elements of a functional structure and of a projected structure , in a hybrid way. "In parallel with the functional structure, project groups are created under the responsibility of functional managers" (CARVALHO and RABECHINI JR., 2009, p. 31).

Fig. 75 - Shows an example of matrix structure. The structures can be light or weak, balanced or balanced and strong. The light structures are close to the functional ones, what differs is that one of the employees (staff) are chosen to manage the project. In the balanced structure the project leader has a certain freedom in management, but answers to the functional manager. The strong matrices, on the other hand, the project manager has total autonomy compared to the functional manager.

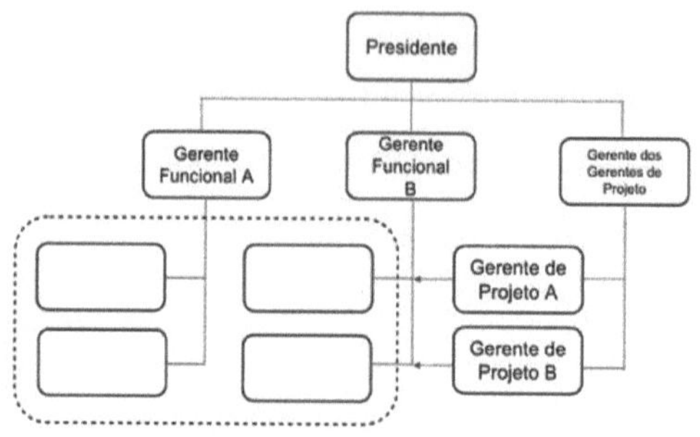

Figure 75 - Matrix structure

Source: Adapted from Veras (2016, p. 76).

Note in Fig. 75, the project manager leads a team according to the functional area staff, however, he is an employee of one of the areas. Influences on this type of structure lead to a certain conflict between the project manager and the functional manager, as resources are shared. In this sense, communication, influences and relationships must be well worked out in order for projects and functional activities to run smoothly.

Understand that in addition to detailed project management planning that is coherent and highly predictable, we also need to identify how the parties involved work within an organisational structure and how we can apply the power of influence to certain organisational structures.

Besides knowing the way of working and the organisational structure where the project and those involved in the project are inserted, it is necessary to draw up a communication plan between the stakeholders.

The communication planning in the project is an artifact that supports the manager and stakeholders in the information during the life cycle of the project and should contain according to Carvalho and Rabechini Jr. (2009) the information that each stakeholder should receive, including format, content and level of detail, in addition to the media technology that the information will be distributed, for example, e-mail, message, etc.. The information among stakeholders must be planned in terms of frequency, in which each stakeholder needs the information in question, and the control for sending and receiving it. An example of a tool to consolidate this information among *stakeholders* is the communication matrix, as shown in Box 32 below:

Table 32 - Matrix of *stakeholders*

Interested	Information	Medium	Frequency (Date/Location)	Control
Senior Management	Present the follow-up of the project	Meeting	weekly	Follow-up and feedback meeting
Development team	Updated schedule	E-mail	weekly	Schedule information
	EAP	Meeting	weekly	Review of deliveries

Source: adapted from CARVALHO and RABECHINI JR (2009)

Stakeholders in the project can be: the project sponsor or project Sponsor (the one who guides, encourages, clarifies the purpose, goals and deliverables, evaluates and approves the project, acting as the main mediator, support and clarifier of the project environment, together with the project manager); different from the project manager, who must orchestrate the realisation of aspects of the project plan such as scope, time, cost, risks, communication; the funder (the person who pays for the project), the beneficiary (is the person or group who will receive the project benefits), the end user (is the person who will use the project deliverables) and the end customer (is the end consumer of the project). The information exchanged between the interested parties can be the information of the artifacts generated in the project. The means of communication used by the interested parties can be a meeting, the sending of an e-mail or even the making of a phone call. The control of communication can be a follow-up by meeting, schedule or a checklist.

Another complementary tool for the project communication fabric, which can be used with the stakeholder matrix, is the responsibility matrix. This new matrix presents the processes or activities linked to the roles of stakeholders. A practical example of a simple software process, referring to Box 33, "Responsibility Matrix", is the software development process and its implementation in an organisation.

In this activity, the business analyst or consultant is responsible for identifying the problem and collecting the client's requirements (Accoutable). At this time, the client is consulted about the availability of the agenda of users who will be interviewed, since he or she will also be informed about the completion of this stage of collecting information for the development of the system. The project manager is informed of the completion of this task, for monitoring and control in the project.

The consultant then carries out a series of tasks of analysis and prior technical feasibility of the client's requirements, in consultation with Sponsor and the systems analyst. The project manager is informed of the execution of this activity.

The next activity to be executed is the planning and development of the commercial proposal or Project Charter, under the joint responsibility of the Sponsor (account provider) and the project manager, where the business analyst is consulted, contributing the information for the assembly of the Project Charter artifact, and the client is informed of this step.

The Project Charter is then presented by the consultant or Business Analyst to the client, obtaining or not the initial approval of the project. The

Sponsor, manager and client/funder must be informed of the opening presentation of the project.

The signing of the initial project proposal, i.e. the initial approval of the project is the responsibility of the client and the CEO of the service provider or, in many cases, of the Sponsor responsible for the project portfolio itself. The business analyst and project manager are informed of the approval.

The next activity now is to detail and transform customer requirements into functional and non-functional requirements, modeling the requirements through diagrams, standardizing them for coding. The responsibility for this task is that of the systems analyst. At this moment the business analyst is consulted to contribute with the necessary information for the coherent modeling and the project manager must be informed or consulted, of the execution of this activity, for the proper monitoring and control of the software metrics. Sponsor can be consulted for support and guidance.

Sequentially, the models are transformed into a coding by the programmer, generating prototypes or ready-made codings, according to the type of software process methodology. The systems analyst is consulted whenever there are doubts about the transformation from modeling to coding. The project manager must be informed or consulted, of the execution of this activity, for the proper monitoring and control of the software metrics. Sponsor can be consulted for support and guidance.

Once the coding has been completed, Tester's role as the software quality determinant now appears. The programmer and the system analyst can be consulted and asked to repair a feature that has been questioned by Tester. As with previous activities, the project manager must be informed and consulted, while Sponsor can be consulted for support and guidance.

After the software goes through the quality stage, the implementation analyst will be responsible for deploying the software to the client and making the appropriate parameterizations. In this sense the system analyst, business analyst and Sponsor are consulted, contributing with technical, business and metric information, respectively. The project manager must be informed or consulted, of the execution of this activity, for the proper monitoring and control of the software metrics.

Finally the users will be trained by the implanter and the system put into production, after the parametrization in pilot, or use of test bases. Sponsor and business analyst can be consulted if necessary, contributing technical and business information. The project manager must be informed of the completion of the software deployment at the customer.

Table 33 - Matrix of responsibility

Processes/ Activities	Papers							
	Business Analyst / Consultant	Systems Analyst	Programmer	Tester	Implantator	Manager	Client / Financier	Sponsor /CEO
Identify the problem and collect the customer's requirements	R/A					I	C	
Analysis of customer requirements	R	C				I		C
Developing the commercial proposal/Project Charter	C					R	I	R/A
Presentation of the proposal	R					I	I	I

Approval of the proposal	I					I	R	R
Modelling the system	C	R		I		I/C		C
Coding the system		C	R			I/C		C
Testing the system		C	C	R		I/C		C
Deploying the system	C	C		I	R	I/C		C
Training the user					R	I/C		C

Therefore, it is vital to understand the organisational structure, control planning, frequency and means of sending information between the parties involved, and planning the roles of the stakeholders within the project. However, the insertion of agile teams in agile projects is of vital importance and efficiency of a software and development project.

2.6.1 Agile teams

Within an agile methodology, building and managing adaptable, disciplined and self-organizing teams is essential for method efficiency and effectiveness. The agile software development process is characterized by the speed of manufacturing useful software, reducing bureaucracy through a few artifacts (documents). Through iterations of execution of activities in short spaces of time (maximum of one month), where it is possible to make changes with the client reducing the risks of the project, thus becoming a "light" project. For Foggetti (2014, p.17) "in a self-organizable team, the professionals assume the responsibility of managing their workload, exchanging tasks among themselves according to each one's capacity to participate in the decision making".

The manager in agile teams has the role of defining a team of the right people, knowing the tools and methods of modeling and communication, such as Canvas and infographics, articulating the whole team so that they have a macro view of the project and detailed product. Therefore, it must focus on communication and collaboration in the foreground and then on documentation.

For Foggetti (2014) besides the communication and collaboration feature, we can list the role of the manager, such as

-To help the team make decisions.

-Create   self-organizing team.

-To encourage   the team to work calmly, even in an environment of change.

-Use the leadership influence gained through respect for the team, through integrity, skill, fairness and trust.

-Delegating decision making to the team, but at the same time must be influencing, facilitating and assisting the team.

Therefore, an agile team manager must be a leader, know his team, transmitting simplicity, simplification, stimulating self-discipline, favouring means for the team to be self organized and collaborative.

We have reached the end of this work and understand the importance of the software development process, and that in each phase it is necessary to implement full quality. Through the management of software projects, the stages of tests and validations, the implementation of quality standards and models that apply the best practices of the software development process, we reach a result of software excellence. I believe that this study is of value and serves as support in the applications of the software development process.

References

AUDY, J.; PRIKLANDNICKI, R. **Distributed Software Development: software development with distributed teams.** Rio de Janeiro: Elsevier. 2008.

BARNEY, J.B.; HESTERLY, W.S. **Strategic management and competitive advantage.** São Paulo: Pearson Prentice Hall, 2011.

BORGES, C.; ROLLIM, F. **Applied Project Management. Concepts and Practical Guide.** Rio de Janeiro: Brasport. 2015. Available in the virtual library.

BROOKSHEAR, J. G. **Computer Science: A Comprehensive View.** 11th Ed. Porto Alegre: Bookman. 2013.

CAMARGO, M. R. **Project Management. Fundamentals and Integrated Practice.** 2nd Ed. Rio de Janeiro: Elsevier. 2018.

CARVALHO, F. C. A. de. **Project Management.** 1st ed. São Paulo: Pearson Education do Brasil, 2015.

CARVALHO, M. M. de. LAURINDO, J. B. **Estratégia competitiva: dos conceitos à implementação.** 2ª Ed. São Paulo: Atlas, 2010.

CARVALHO, M. M.; RABECHINI, Jr., R. **Building project management skills: theory and cases.** São Paulo: Atlas, 2009.

CAVALCANTI, M.; FARAH, O. E.; MARCONDES, L. P. (Org.). **Strategic Business Management.** 3. ed. São Paulo: Cengage, 2018.

CHIAVENATO, I. **Introduction to General Theory of Administration: a comprehensive view of modern management of organisations: compact edition.** 3. ed. Rio de Janeiro: Elsevier, 2004.

CHIAVENATO, I. **General and public administration.** Rio de Janeiro: Elsevier, 2006.

CIERCO, A.; MONAT, A. S.; NASCIMENTO, F. P.; MENDES, J. R. B. **Project Management.** Rio de Janeiro: Editora FGV. 2012.

CRUZ, F. **Scrum and Agile in Projects: Complete Guide.** Rio de Janeiro: Brasport. 2015.

CRUZ, F. **Scrum and PMBOK Guide united in project management.** Rio de Janeiro: Brasport. 2013.

DAYCHOUM, M. **40+16 management tools and techniques.** Rio de Janeiro: Brasport. 2016.

ENGHOLM JÚNIOR, H. **Software Engineering in practice.** São Paulo: Novatec Editora. 2010.

FAGUNDES, P.B. **Framework for comparison and analysis of agile methods. Dissertation.** UFSC. 2005. Available at:
<
https://repositorio.ufsc.br/bitstream/handle/123456789/101860/220977.pdf?sequence=1&isAllowed=y>. Accessed: 18 August 2020.

FEATHERS, M. C. **Effective Work with Legacy Code.** Porto Alegre: AMGH, 2013.

FOGGETTI, C. **Agile Project Management.** São Paulo: Education do Brasil, 2014.

FREEMAN, R. **Oracle, reference for DBA: essential techniques for DBA daily life.** Rio de Janeiro: Elsevier. 2005.

FREZATTI, F. **Orçamento Empresarial: planning and management control.** São Paulo: Atlas, 2009.

GAMMA, E et al. **Standards Design: reusable object oriented software solutions.** Porto Alegre: Bookman, 2000.

GOMES, A. F. **Agile: software development with frequent deliveries and focus on business value.** Home of the Code. 2014.

GONÇALVES, R. R. **Economic Scenarios and Trends.** Rio de Janeiro: FGV Editorial, 2011.

GRONOVICZ, M. A. et. al. **Lean Office: A project office application. Magazine Gestão e Conhecimento**, v.7, n.1, jan./jun. p. 48-74, 2013.

HELDMAN, K. **Project Management: Guide to the official PMI examination.** Rio de Janeiro: Elsevier. 2006.

HIRAMA, K. **Software Engineering: quality and productivity with technology.** Rio de Janeiro: Elsevier. 2012.

IIBA. **A Guide to the Body of Business Analysis Knowledge (BABOK Guide): version 2.0.** International Institute of Business Analysis. 2011.

JACOBS, F. R.; CHASE, R.B. **Operations and Supply Chain Management.** 13th ed. AMGH Editora. 2009.

JUNGED, D.; BARBALHO, S. C. M.; SILVA, S. L. **Project Management. Theory, Practice and Trends.** Rio de Janeiro: Elsevier, 2014.

KERIEVSKY, J. **Refactoring for Standards.** Porto Alegre: Bookman, 2008.

KOSCIANSKI, A.; SOARES, M. dos S. **Software Quality.** Learn more modern methodologies and techniques for software development. 2nd ed. São Paulo: Novatec Editora. 2007.

LESSA, R. O.; LESSA JUNIOR, E. **O. Software engineering process models.** Scientific article. 2009.

LINDERS, B. **Combining Agile and Lean approaches.** Available at: https://www.infoq.com/br/news/2014/02/combinando-agile-lean. Accessed September 24, 2017.

http://xps-project.googlecode.com/svn-history/r43/trunk/outros/02_Artigo.pdf

MARTINS, J. C. C. **Software Development Project Management with PMI, RUP and UML.** Rio de Janeiro: Brasport. 2010.

MARITNS, J. C. C. **Techniques for Software Project Management.** Rio de Janeiro: Brasport. 2007.

MARTIM, R.; MARTIM, M. **Principle, Standards and Agile Practices in C#.** Porto Alegre: Bookman, 2011.

MASSARI, V. **Agile Scrum Master in Advanced Project Management.** Rio de Janeiro: Brasport. 2016.

MAXIMILIAN, A. C. A. **Project Management. How to Turn Ideas into Results.** 4th Edition. Atlas Publishing. 2010.

MONTEIRO, A. **PMP Certification: optimise your study time in preparation for the PMP certification exam: focus your studies on the most charged topics in the certification exams: issues solved and commented.** Rio de Janeiro. Brasport. 2008

MUNIZ JUNIOR, J.; et. al. **Production Administration.** IESDE BRASIL S.A. 2012.

MEI, P. Pm Mind Map. **The uncomplicated management of projects.** Rio de Janeiro: Brasport. 2015. Available in the Virtual Library

NEVES, M. **CBAP Master: Learn business analysis and achieve CCBA/CBAP certification.** Rio de Janeiro: Brasport. 2014.

NORO, G. de B. **The management of Stakeholders in Project Management. GEP - Project Management Magazine.** V3. n. 1. p. 127-158. Jan/Apr. São Paulo. 2012.

OGC - **Office of Government Commerce. Gerenciando Projetos de Sucesso com PRINCE2.** TSO (The Stationery Office). 2011.

Available at:
<https://books.google.com.br/books?id=1wFOljsw5bgC&printsec=frontcover &dq=prince2&hl=ptBR&sa=X&ved=0ahUKEwitxdKHksPpAhWaILkGHQM ADOYQ6AEIKzAA#v=onepage&q=prince2&f=false>. Accessed 23 May 2020.

OLIVEIRA, O. J. **Management of qualidade : advanced topics.** 2012.

ORTH, A. I. ; PRIKLANDNICKI, R. **Project planning and management.** Porto Alegre: EDIPUCRS. 2009.

PIRES, W. S. **Project Management using agile methods: theory and practice.** 1st edition of Belo Horizonte: Authors' Club. 2016.

PMBOK. **Project Management Body Knowledge - Project Management Knowledge.** (PMBOK Guide). 5th Edition. PMI. 2013.

POSSI, M. **Project Management professional's guide: volume 1: general approach and scope definition.** Rivers of January: Brasport. 2006.

PRIKLANDNICKI, R.; WILLI, R.; MILANI, F. **Agile methods for software development.** Porto Alegre: Bookman. 2014.

PRESSMAN, R. S.; MAXIM, B. R. **Software Engineering. A professional approach.** 8th Ed. Porto Alegre: AMGH. 2016.

PIZE, A. **Strategic Project Planning and Alignment: A practical guide applying the SPCanvas and PSACanvas models.** São Paulo: Brasport. 2015.

PROPPENDIECK, M.; PROPPENDIECK, T. **Implementing Lean Software Development: From concept to money.** Bookman. RABECHINI JUNIOR, R.; CARVALHO, M. M. de. **Project Management in Practice: Brazilian Cases.** 1st ed. São Paulo: Atlas, 2013. 2011.

REZENDE, D. A. **Software Engineering and Information Systems.** Rio de Janeiro: Brasport. 2005.

SCHACH, S. R. **Software Engineering: The Classic & Object Oriented Paradigms.** 7th Ed. Porto Alegre. AMGH. 2010.

SLACK, N.; CHAMBERS, S.; JOHNSTON, R.; BETTS, A. **Operations and Process Management. Principles and practices of strategic impact.** Bookman, 2013.

SCHIRIGATTI, J.L. **Database Systems.** Beau Bassin-Rose Hill; Mauritius, New Academic Editions, 2020.

STELLMAN, A.; GREENE, J. **Use the Head! Agile.** Rio de Janeiro: Alta Books, 2019.

SOARES, M. dos S. **Metodologias Ágeis Extreme Programming e Scrum para Desenvolvimento de Software.** Electronic Magazine of Information Systems. V.15. n.3. sep - dec. 2016.

SOMMERVILLE, I. **Software Engineering.** São Paulo: Pearson Prentice Hall. 2011.

VARGAS, R. V. **Project Management: establishing competitive differentials.** 8th ed. Rio de Janeiro: Brasport. 2016.

VAZQUEZ, C. E. SIMÕES, G. S. **Requirements Engineering: business oriented software.** Rio de Janeiro: Brasport. 2016.

VERAS, M. **Dynamic Project Management: LifeCycle Canvas.** Rio de Janeiro: Brasport. 2016.

XAVIER, C. M. of S. **Project Management: how to define and control the scope of the project.** 3rd ed. São Paulo: Saraiva, 2016.

ZACCARELLI, S. B. **Strategy and Success in Business.** São Paulo: Saraiva, 2012.

Printed by Books on Demand GmbH, Norderstedt / Germany